Dear World Leader,

Hard Rain has been sent to every prime minister and president in the .... global problems you were elected to solve: poverty, the wasteful use of resources, pollution, the loss of habitats and species, and the summation of our problems, climate change. This book and the exhibition that is touring the world are designed to help generate public support to decarbonize energy, pass legislation that gives companies the security to invest in ever-cleaner technology, and develop equitable trade agreements that allow poor countries to eliminate persistent pockets of poverty. Fifty years ago the UN set a target of 0.7% of GDP as official aid. Up to now, only five countries have met that target. Aid is needed to support education for girls and boys and provide child healthcare and family planning programmes. These measures are in all our interests. Humanity shares a common fate on a crowded planet.

The problems highlighted in Hard Rain are understood by decision-makers, but they typically continue to be addressed as separate issues. Climate change is handcuffed to poverty, which is linked to all the problems illustrated in this book. It must now be clear that the world needs to tackle all of these issues together if we are to solve any of them.

We are not going to pretend that there are solutions to all our problems. Many scientists and environmental experts acknowledge that there is a price to pay for the delay in dealing with them. There is disagreement about the exact price for the damage we have done to the earth's life-support systems, but all are agreed that every step we take towards a sustainable future will lessen the impact of a natural backlash that will damage civilization and nature.

Hard Rain is an appeal to you and an appeal to readers to get in touch with you to support your government's efforts to lead your country towards forms of progress that sustain all of humanity, while sustaining the planet.

This project began forty years ago on the day of the first moon landing, when I was lost in the Sahara and rescued by a Tuareg nomad who played me "A Hard Rain's A-Gonna Fall". "Sad forests", "dead oceans", "Where the people are many and their hands are all empty", "Where hunger is ugly, where souls are forgotten": I have seen Bob Dylan's piercing words come alive in the viewfinder of my camera and in the photographs of my friends. It has fallen to our generation to deal with these tragic problems that now threaten to overwhelm us all.

I welcome your response to Hard Rain and will be pleased to add your comments to those from heads of state already posted on our website.

Sincerely,

Mark Edwards

HARD RAIN PROJECT

Hard Rain Project
199 Shooters Hill Road
London SE3 8UL
United Kingdom

T: +44 (0)20 8858 8307
E: mark@hardrainproject.com
www.hardrainproject.com

*You cannot solve the problem
with the same kind of thinking
that has created the problem.*

Albert Einstein

HARD RAIN

OUR HEADLONG COLLISION WITH NATURE

Mark Edwards
Lyric by Bob Dylan

First edition published in Great Britain in 2006 by
Still Pictures Moving Words Ltd
199 Shooters Hill Road
London SE3 8UL, UK

Third edition published in 2009

10 9 8 7 6 5 4 3 2 1

A catalogue record for this book is available from the British Library

ISBN 978-1-905588-02-2

Design Bailey and Kenny
Managing editor Mark Reynolds
Printed by Beacon Press, Uckfield

This book is dedicated to my incandescent god-daughter Alice Jacoby

I owe a lot more than thanks to the Tuareg nomad who rescued me, and to Bob Dylan who gave permission to publish "A Hard Rain's A-Gonna Fall".

Many of the staff at Sony/ATV Music Publishing have helped this project on its journey from an idea in the desert to a book and touring exhibition. I am very grateful to Rakesh Sanghvi, Janice Brock, Mark Waring and Gary Bhupsingh.

Charlie Stanford at Columbia Records, London, encouraged me to roll the exhibition out around the world. His help and support have been invaluable.

The photographs in Hard Rain are sourced from Still Pictures, the London bureau of a unique worldwide network of photo agencies with well over a million images available to publishers, NGOs, governments and UN agencies. Our combined collection, which includes the photo archive of the United Nations Environment Programme, has earned a reputation as the leading source of images that illustrate environment and development issues, nature and wildlife. Special thanks to our key partners: Catherine Deulofeu at BIOS in France, Peter Arnold at Peter Arnold Inc in the US, Steve Jackson at UNEP in Kenya and Hartmut Schwarzbach and Peter Frischmuth at Argus in Germany.

Contents

Lost

It's July 20th, 1969 – Apollo 11 mission to the moon. Buzz Aldrin's planting an American flag in a lunar crater. I'm lost in the Sahara Desert, about to be rescued by a Tuareg nomad – an Omar Sharif look-alike who rode out of the mirage – real life imitating David Lean's *Lawrence of Arabia*.

He takes me to his people, sits me down on a rock – it turns out to be part of a fossilized tree trunk – and disappears into a tiny hut. My companion reappears with a rolled umbrella, two sticks and a cassette player. He rubs the sticks together, makes a fire, boils a pot of water, and we have a nice cup of tea. I'm unnerved by uncomplicated kindliness. Then he warms the batteries in the cassette player, turns it on and Bob Dylan sings "A Hard Rain's A-Gonna Fall".

My heart sinks. I've spent three years at art school keeping out of range of Dylan's early folk albums and here I am practically a captive audience[1]. But the urgency of Dylan's voice, the sheer intensity of communication in the coming-together of words and guitar cut through my prejudice and I get it. In "A Hard Rain's A-Gonna Fall", Dylan lifts the heart of popular music from sheer entertainment to art.

I'm in the front row of an astonishing concert of human contradictions, sitting on a tree turned to rock by a change in the climate millions of years ago.

The crew of Apollo 11 are sending back photographs of the earth from space. We had the whole wide world in our hands. The newspapers wrote about our fragile, lonely, blue planet while we trashed it with no thought for the future.

I'm surrounded by dignified, graceful people from another age, warmed against the surprising chill of the night by a fire lit by friction – our first step to a scientific, industrial society, to putting men on the moon. And to changing the climate.

Bob Dylan's song of love and death and dying life is burning into me. As Dylan piles image upon image, I have the idea to illustrate each line of the lyric.

In the following years I travelled to over 150 countries to photograph our headlong collision with nature. And here it is – Bob Dylan's piercing words as I saw them in the viewfinder of my camera, completed with pictures by my friends.

Mark Edwards
London, July 20th, 2009

[1] What a stick-in-the-mud I was in my early twenties. I discovered Dylan on *Highway 61*, writing and singing like no one before or since. I wanted him at the frontier, live and dangerous – not singing weird old songs. I was just like the folk-music purists who wanted him for themselves, safe within the confines of their tradition. How fortunate for us all that Dylan stayed true to his own imagination.

A Hard Rain's A-Gonna Fall

Oh, where have you been, my blue-eyed son?
Oh, where have you been, my darling young one?

I've stumbled on the side of twelve misty mountains

I've walked and I've crawled on six crooked highways

I've stepped in the middle of seven sad forests

I've been out in front of a dozen dead oceans

I've been ten thousand miles in the mouth of a graveyard

And it's a hard, and it's a hard, it's a hard, and it's a hard,
And it's a hard rain's a-gonna fall.

Oh, what did you see, my blue-eyed son?
Oh, what did you see, my darling young one?

I saw a newborn baby with wild wolves all around it

I saw a highway of diamonds with nobody on it

I saw a black branch with blood that kept drippin'

I saw a room full of men with their hammers a-bleedin'

I saw a white ladder all covered with water

I saw ten thousand talkers whose tongues were all broken

I saw guns and sharp swords in the hands of young children

And it's a hard, and it's a hard, it's a hard, it's a hard,
And it's a hard rain's a-gonna fall.

And what did you hear, my blue-eyed son?
And what did you hear, my darling young one?

I heard the sound of a thunder, it roared out a warnin'

Heard the roar of a wave that could drown the whole world

Heard one hundred drummers whose hands were a-blazin'

Heard ten thousand whisperin' and nobody listenin'

Heard one person starve, I heard many people laughin'

Heard the song of a poet who died in the gutter

Heard the sound of a clown who cried in the alley

And it's a hard, and it's a hard, it's a hard, it's a hard,
And it's a hard rain's a-gonna fall.

Oh, who did you meet, my blue-eyed son?
Who did you meet, my darling young one?

I met a young child beside a dead pony

I met a white man who walked a black dog

I met a young woman whose body was burning

I met a young girl, she gave me a rainbow

I met one man who was wounded in love

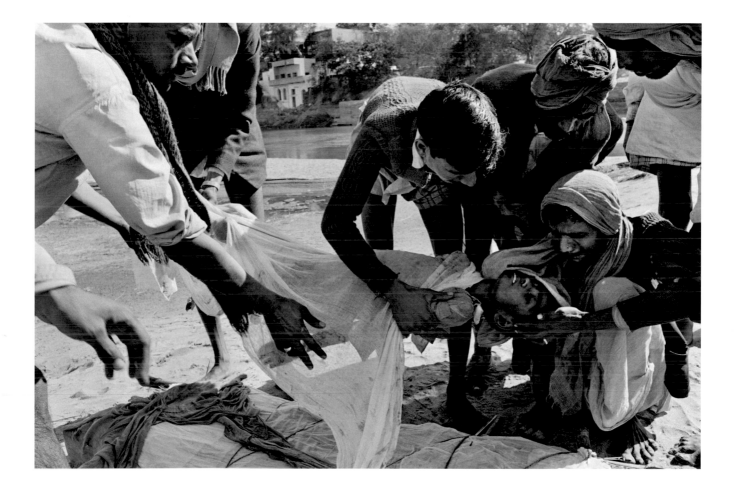

I met another man who was wounded with hatred

And it's a hard, it's a hard, it's a hard, it's a hard,
It's a hard rain's a-gonna fall.

Oh, what'll you do now, my blue-eyed son?
Oh, what'll you do now, my darling young one?

I'm a-goin' back out 'fore the rain starts a-fallin'

I'll walk to the depths of the deepest black forest

Where the people are many and their hands are all empty

Where the pellets of poison are flooding their waters

Where the home in the valley meets the damp dirty prison

Where the executioner's face is always well hidden

Where hunger is ugly, where souls are forgotten

Where black is the color, where none is the number

And I'll tell it and think it and speak it and breathe it

And reflect it from the mountain so all souls can see it

Then I'll stand on the ocean until I start sinkin'

But I'll know my song well before I start singin'

And it's a hard, it's a hard, it's a hard, it's a hard,
It's a hard rain's a-gonna fall.

COMMENTARIES

"I wrote it at the time of the Cuban crisis. I was in Bleecker Street in New York. We just hung around at night – people sat around wondering if it was the end, and so did I. Would 10 o'clock the next day ever come?... It was a song of desperation. What could we do? Could we control the men on the verge of wiping us out? The words came fast – very fast. It was a song of terror. Line after line, trying to capture the feeling of nothingness."
Bob Dylan

"A Hard Rain's A-Gonna Fall" is our most powerful reminder of the fear Dylan's generation experienced at the prospect of life ending in nuclear war. But as Clinton Heylin writes in *Behind the Shades*, Dylan has been at pains to point out that this song has a broader sweep, a wider meaning, one appropriate before, during and after the Cuban missile crisis.

The environmental crisis is just as desperate and just as threatening as nuclear wipeout. Dylan's question, only slightly reframed, is exactly right: can we influence the people in power to deal with our problems?

The issues highlighted in Hard Rain – the wasteful and unsustainable use of resources by the few, debilitating poverty for the many, population expansion, habitat loss, species extinction, and the summation of our problems, climate change – are like pieces of a jigsaw puzzle that illustrate the 21st century.

If we put the puzzle together we see that there are not many problems but one problem: aligning human systems with natural systems. A few examples show how these issues are all linked by cause and effect. Unsustainable logging of rainforests opens up jungles to commercial and subsistence farmers, who burn more forest to expand agricultural land. Almost 20% of global CO_2 pollution is added to the atmosphere from burning forests. Much of the deforested land is used to grow soya beans to feed farm animals, which in turn feed expanding human populations. Livestock add methane – a potent greenhouse gas – to the atmosphere, which

combines with CO_2 from power stations and the engines that drive us and our goods around the world. These greenhouse gases are heating the planet with untold consequences. Forest destruction also accelerates species loss, damaging the web of life that we depend on for clean air, water and food.

While each of these issues is understood by decision-makers, they are typically addressed as if they were separate problems. We will be wise to look upon ourselves as a species and devise more realistic and pragmatic approaches to all our problems as a whole.

The fault is not just with our leaders – we all have to take responsibility for the colossal mess we have made in the world. We have to acknowledge that up to now we have been heralding weak and largely substanceless global accords as great achievements[1]. Our quiet clamour for hypocrisy and deception, for schemes that seem to promise something for nothing, has not produced solutions. We have to give governments a constituency to reinvent the modern world so that it is sustainable. This is the biggest project humanity has ever faced.

We need to act quickly. The localized climate-related disasters that we read about every day could begin to occur across the planet if a runaway, irreversible greenhouse effect kicks in. If we wait for more disasters like continental droughts (already happening in Australia), plagues of tropical diseases in places not strictly tropical, massive hurricanes and typhoons flattening major cities, then governments will panic and pass panic-inspired laws and regulations.

[1] Stephen Gardiner, "A Perfect Moral Storm: Climate change, intergenerational ethics and the problem of corruption", in *Environmental Values* 15, 2006

Democracy and diverse approaches could be early victims of global warming.

As David Skitt has commented (see pages 149–50) what this present point in history demands, according to a recent UK government report on climate change, is "unprecedented international cooperation", nothing less than a new human mentality – one that transcends our neurotically obsessive allegiances to national interests and identity. Old ways of thinking don't work any more. And it will need a real mental leap to change them. Are we capable of making that leap?

Political change comes only when people form a movement so large that governments have no choice but to listen. This requires a coalition of environmentalists, those in the peace movement, the faith community, those who support the campaign against poverty, and the silent majority. If you are part of the silent majority, now is the time to find your voice.

But we all need to be aware that it's not just political action that is needed. Most of us have lost touch with nature and we need to reconnect with the natural world. Not through photographs, which however beautiful or dramatic are just signposts to reality. This is the first and last step to a sustainable culture that we can all participate in.

The modern philosopher J. Krishnamurti makes the connection between human nature and nature in this passage from *All the Marvelous Earth*:

"There is a tree by the river and we have been watching it day after day for several weeks when the sun is beginning to rise. As the sun rises slowly over the horizon, over the trees, this particular tree becomes all of a sudden golden. All the leaves are bright with life, and as you watch them as the hours pass by, that tree whose name does not matter – what matters is that beautiful tree – an extraordinary quality seems to spread over the land, over the river... Towards evening when the western skies are lit up by the setting sun, the tree gradually becomes sombre, dark, closing in on itself. The sky has become red, yellow, green, but the tree remains quiet, hidden, and is resting for the night.

"If you establish a relationship with it, then you have a relationship with mankind. You are responsible then for that tree and for the trees of the world. But if you have no relationship with the living things on this earth, you may lose whatever relationship you have with humanity, with human beings."

Kathmandu, Nepal, Christmas Day 1970 and the same view thirty years later

In 1970 it was mist over the mountains, now it's smog. The earth has been transformed by human activities – from a planet dominated by rural populations to one dominated by cities. Forty years ago Kathmandu had barely 200,000 inhabitants. When the second picture was taken, its population had swelled to over a million. For the first time in human history as many people live in an urban environment as in a rural one. Most new urbanites live in illegal shanty towns, where they demonstrate great ingenuity in coping with incredibly difficult circumstances.

Urbanization presents an opportunity to tackle poverty that would not be possible in a rural setting. In cities it is easier to provide greater numbers of people with education, health services, jobs, shelter and family planning services that together could help slow population growth.

In *Hot, Flat and Crowded*, Thomas L. Friedman asks readers to imagine tapping into the creativity and innovative capacity of the world's poorest people. I've been fortunate to spend time in shanty towns so I've got some idea of the explosion of innovation we might expect in science and technology, art and literature if it were possible to provide the tools and energy people need to compete, connect and collaborate.

Bangladeshi refugees, Calcutta, India

I took this profoundly disturbing picture of a man carrying his cholera-stricken wife during the Bangladesh war in 1971. Ten million people crossed the East Pakistan border into India to escape the horrors of this bloody war.

Photographs are a shadow of the past but they can also be a ghost of the future. If we go on trapping the sun's heat in the atmosphere by burning fossil fuels, ice on land will melt, eventually causing sea levels to rise – potentially by 20 metres.

If the sea level rose by just one metre it would make 20 million people homeless in Bangladesh and India alone. Where will they go? Hands up the country that will take in 20 million refugees as their own coastlines are being breached by rising seas, as agriculture fails, as clean water becomes scarce, as law and order break down. There is nowhere for 20 million people to go.

Forest destruction, Haiti

Some 500 years ago, Christopher Columbus discovered the island of Hispaniola, now divided between Haiti and the Dominican Republic. This is how he described his first view of the island.

> Its lands are high, there are in it many sierras and very lofty mountains... All are most beautiful, of a thousand shapes: all are accessible and filled with trees of a thousand kinds and tall, so that they seem to touch the sky. I am told that they never lose their foliage, and this I can believe, for I saw them as green and lovely as they are in Spain in May, and some bearing fruit, and some at another stage, according to their nature.

The photograph shows what that landscape looks like today. The great forests have been cut down and much of the topsoil has washed into the sea, guaranteeing continued poverty.

In his essay in the first edition of Hard Rain, Lloyd Timberlake makes the link between poverty and environmental destruction and shows how rich nations keep poor countries poor: "Poor people simply cannot live sustainably and they are forced to overuse and degrade scarce resources, whether firewood or topsoil, or water in arid areas. Countries with majorities of poor citizens cannot afford honest, effective government, infrastructure such as roads and communications systems, and healthcare. Thus they do not attract foreign investment. It is as hard for a poor country to pull itself out of poverty as for a poor person.

"The wealthier countries have actually developed policies that keep poor countries poor. They mostly come in the form of rich countries using their muscle and wealth to keep weaker, poorer countries from competing with them. The US and Europe pay their rich farmers $300 billion a year to overproduce commodities such as cotton and sugar, thereby lowering world prices for poor farmers in poor countries. When international treaties are negotiated, rich countries send delegations of dozens of lawyers and experts, overwhelming the one or two delegates poor countries can afford or find."

Oiled bird, Brazil
© D. Rodrigues/UNEP/Still Pictures

We learn a lot about big environmental disasters but we may overlook the pollution we ourselves cause. Lights left on in empty rooms, car journeys that could have been cycle rides, heat pouring out of badly insulated homes, shopping taken home in single-use plastic bags. Our small acts of pollution lack the awful drama of the oil spill that trapped this bird but, taken together, they are far more destructive to the planet. Ten times more oil reaches the seas from car owners pouring old engine oil down drains than from oil tanker disasters like this one off the coast of Brazil that polluted miles of coastline and killed thousands of seabirds.

It's easy to be paralyzed by the scale of our environmental problems, but as individuals we can act immediately to reduce our environmental footprint. This sends a powerful signal to politicians and business leaders. Edmund Burke once famously said, "Nobody made a greater mistake than he who did nothing because he could do only a little." But what a lot some people do. Wildlife filmmaker Rebecca Hosking was moved to tears by the impact of plastic rubbish on marine life when she was filming off Hawaii. When she returned home, she showed shopkeepers in her town the film she had made. As a result Modbury in Devon became the first town in Europe to be entirely free of plastic bags. Shoppers receive their goods in 100% biodegradable cornstarch bags, recyclable paper bags or reusable cotton and jute bags, supplied by a company in neighbouring Cornwall. Working at an even larger scale, Wangari Maathai, "The Tree Mother of Africa", founded the Green Belt Movement, which has planted over 40 million trees across Kenya to prevent soil erosion. She now spearheads the United Nations Environment Programme's Billion Tree Campaign.

Governments have the key role in solving global problems but individuals – all of us – can also have significant impacts.

Taj Mahal, India

A body washed up behind the world's most famous tomb, the Taj Mahal, built to commemorate the death of Shah Jahan's favourite wife, Mumtaz Mahal. The family of the deceased could not afford wood for a funeral pyre. Great wealth and desperate poverty still exist side by side.

Jeffrey Sachs told his 2007 BBC Reith Lecture audience: "The end of poverty – by the year 2025. It seems like an outlandish claim, an impossible dream. But it's within reach. It is a scientifically sound objective. And it is the most urgent challenge of our generation. In fact, if we in the rich world fail to take up this challenge, we will imperil the world and ourselves. A crowded world, one that is 'bursting at the seams', cannot afford to leave millions to die each year of extreme poverty without imperilling all the rest."

Only five countries – Denmark, Luxembourg, the Netherlands, Norway and Sweden – deliver the target of 0.7% of GNP as official aid set out by the UN fifty years ago.

Hard rain, Port au Prince, Haiti

It all begins with a few thin clouds in the clear blue sky over the Indian Ocean. They are barely noticeable at first as the wind picks up and water vapour condenses to form tiny cloud droplets, and the droplets bump into each other and coalesce. The clouds grow and darken. Thunder claps and the first giant raindrops fall on the southern tip of India. The monsoon, the planet's greatest annual weather system, has begun its magic. The clouds sweep north across the subcontinent, enveloping the land in curtains of rain and bringing relief to a parched and overheated soil. In about a hundred hours spread over a hundred days, millions of villages across India receive virtually their only rain of the year.

The rain swells rivers, floods low-lying land, fills reservoirs and irrigation canals, turns deserts green and brings crops to life. The water percolates through the soil to fill the pores in rocks beneath. In the Himalayan mountains, the rains combine with melting waters from ancient glaciers to feed great rivers like the Ganges, the Brahmaputra and the Indus. As the first rains come each June, Indians rush into the streets and party. They put on festivals for their Hindu water gods. They head for their fields to plant crops in the damp soil. They clear debris from ancient channels that divert the precious rains into ponds and lakes – anywhere that they can store the life-giving waters.

The rituals of the monsoon are repeated all across Asia. The first rains are a time for celebration and thanksgiving. In Southeast Asia, fishermen and farmers wait for the first spring flows to revive the Mekong. In China, the Yangtze River brings waters that will feed more than a billion people. In the Americas, under different weather systems, farmers watch the skies for the first sign of storms forming in the Caribbean. In Africa, there is special nervousness. If the rains fail, it can mean famine and starvation. But everywhere people instinctively know the truth of Benjamin Franklin's famous saying: "When the well's dry, we know the worth of water."

Water is our most fundamental natural resource. We cannot survive without it. But it is also our most renewable resource. Those clouds forming over the Indian Ocean are just the latest step in a never-ending water cycle. The stuff we drink today is the same water that the first fish swam in, that the dinosaurs drank and that froze across much of the globe during the ice ages. Our planet probably has no more and no less than it has ever had. Each day some 800 billion cubic metres evaporate from the oceans or the land to keep the water cycle in motion. On average it stays in the air for ten days before falling again as rain.

But from the High Andes to the plains of India, from southern Europe to northern China, rain is becoming increasingly unpredictable. Global warming is pumping more energy into weather systems and making them more intense, and that can bring both floods and droughts. In some places, rivers are running dry as rains fail and we take ever more water to irrigate our crops. Conflicts over remaining supplies loom. In other places, warmer air is making storm clouds more intense and generating super-storms and hurricanes. Hard rains are creating havoc.

And yet, in some parts of the world, there are times when there is not enough water. Underground reserves that farmers could once reach by dropping a bucket into a well only a few feet deep are now so empty that a borehole drilled half a mile down finds no water. The great rivers we heard about in our geography lessons in school – strong blue lines on our atlas maps – are running dry. The Nile in Egypt, the Ganges in India and Bangladesh, the Indus in Pakistan, the Yellow River in China and the Colorado in the US are among them. It is not that nature's water cycle is faltering. Far from it. But in some countries our demands on it are increasing so much that we sometimes run out of it.

The dams and irrigation canals of 20th-century engineering are failing. Instead, many communities are going back to traditional ways of managing water. They are harvesting the rains and diverting floodwaters into wells to save it for the next drought.

Fred Pearce

A child suffering from malnutrition, Haiti

"How much is that doggy in the window?" Well, now we know. If it's an American dog it's equivalent, ecologically speaking, to a dozen Bangladeshi or African children. As the Derek Wall of the Green Party of England and Wales points out, cats in the rich world have more power and influence than the poor people of this planet. Accidents of geography and genes should no longer determine who gets the fish.

Melt lake, Greenland
© Uriel Sinai/Getty Images

Warmer air temperatures are causing the Greenland ice sheet to melt earlier and faster than previously anticipated. Once the ice starts to melt at the surface, it forms lakes and rivers. Melt water drains through the cracks, creating a layer between the bottom of the ice and the rock below, slightly lifting it and moving it towards the sea as if on a conveyor belt. Additionally, warm ocean waters are destabilizing the mouths of outlet glaciers, further accelerating their flow. The giant Jakobshavn Glacier on Greenland's west coast is advancing towards the sea twice as fast as a decade ago at 12 kilometres per year, or over 30 metres per day. The amount of fresh water entering the oceans around Greenland has tripled in the same period. Were Greenland to lose its ice cap, an area almost as large as Mexico, the world's oceans would rise by six metres and flood large parts of just about every coastal city on the planet. If our governments don't cooperate to reduce greenhouse gases, we will have to redraw the map of the world continually as coastlines erode.

Our modern world is delicate and finely balanced, ecologically and economically; a seemingly insignificant change could trigger a process known as positive feedback in the climate. If this happens, global warming itself would precipitate alterations in the earth's natural systems, causing additional warming, which in turn would bring about yet more changes – an unstoppable acceleration that could transform the planet.

Amazon jungle being burned to expand agricultural land, Brazil
© John Maier/Still Pictures

In the next 24 hours, deforestation will release as much CO_2 into the atmosphere as eight million people flying from London to New York. Deforestation accounts for up to 20% of global CO_2 emissions – more than all the cars, trucks, planes, trains and ships in the world.

What drives the destruction? Trees are cut down for timber and the deforested areas are turned into ranch land, or into farms to grow crops such as soya beans to feed battery chickens and other meat producing animals for our supermarkets. Up to 80% of the world's forests have already been lost or converted to other uses, so time is running out.

No new technology is required to reduce these catastrophic emissions from the forests. This is a victory still waiting to be claimed by politicians. They would need to negotiate a forest charter adding value to standing forests which would counter the power of rising global demand for agricultural land and timber.

Abattoir, England
© Nigel Dickinson/Still Pictures

One of the 4.5 million British cattle suspected of having Bovine Spongiform Encephalopathy, almost certainly caused by BSE-contaminated cattle feed prepared from bovine tissues.

The majority of the animals raised for food live miserable lives in intensive confinement in factory farms. They are pumped full of antibiotics, hormones and other chemicals to encourage high productivity. In the food industry, animals are often treated not as living creatures, but as food-producing machines, and are confined to small cages with metal bars where they breathe ammonia-filled air in artificial lighting or no lighting at all.

English country church

"And God blessed them, and God said to them, Be fruitful and multiply, and fill the earth and subdue it; and have dominion over the fish of the sea and over the birds of the air and over every living thing that moves upon the earth."
Genesis 1:2

If the animals could speak, they would point out that the West has been uniquely irresponsible in the use and treatment of nature and natural resources. We treat nature like a master treats a slave. We have forgotten that we are part of nature, that human is just a word for a species of animal.

In the damaged environment, we glimpse the limits of the modern world. We can see ourselves dependent on nature's extraordinary diversity, which defies the elementary mechanism we have tried to impose. Our arrogant simplicity has been challenged by nature's awesome, but delicate complexity.

Political prisoners tortured to death by the Pol Pot regime, Cambodia
© Mike Kolloffel/Still Pictures

This photograph is a painful reminder that there's always somewhere in the world where cruelty by man against man is performed with organized precision on a scale beyond imagination.

It is not enough just to respond to our environmental problems. We also need to ensure that people have the right to voice their beliefs freely without fear of abuse or punishment.

Child with toy gun, Bucharest, Romania

What starts out as cops and robbers or cowboys and Indians when we are kids may turn into a terrible reality when we are grown up. We've lurched into the 21st century – on the one hand killing and maiming and destroying and on the other trying to find a new, sustainable approach to living harmoniously with nature and ourselves. Two hundred and thirty million people died as a result of war in the 20th century. But I could say it like this: 230 million of us were destroyed by fellow humans. There is no them and us. There's only us. If we don't get that, we don't get sustainability. At the heart of our environmental concern lies an unspoken challenge: to rediscover the reality of interdependence.

I was arrested for taking this photograph and taken to prison by the soldier pointing angrily at me. As I was being handcuffed, an elderly man in ragged clothes came up to me and whispered these lines from *Measure for Measure* in my ear:

> But man, proud man,
> Drest in a little brief authority,
> Most ignorant of what he's most assur'd,
> His glassy essence, like an angry ape,
> Plays such fantastic tricks before high heaven,
> As make the angels weep.

The story ended happily when the prison authorities discovered that I had an invitation to meet Nicolae Ceausescu in Bucharest that evening. I went from prison to palace like a character in the *Arabian Nights*. Shakespeare's lines stayed with me as I stood in line to shake hands with Romania's dictator and they find an echo in the pictures that illustrate this book.

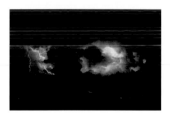

Thunderstorm, Wisconsin, USA
© Keith Kent/Peter Arnold Inc/Still Pictures

I carry an Old Testament image of the moment of creation in my imagination. This astonishing, beautiful photograph brings it alive and with it the knowledge that you and I, and all of us in the rich world, are inadvertently destroying life on earth.

People aren't sitting around saying, "Let's destroy the rainforests, cook the planet, pollute the oceans and damage the ozone layer". These unintended effects are a warning that we have to change how we think and how we live. Our mastery of science has allowed us to break the first law of nature. In nature everything that dies becomes the starting point for new growth. A leaf falls from a tree, is broken down by plant cells and the nutrients are reabsorbed to become part of next year's growth. In the last fifty years we have made materials and chemicals that can't be broken down by plant cells, so they build up in the environment, in landfill sites, in the bodies of wild animals in the remotest parts of the world and in our bodies. Every pregnant woman has on average eight kinds of pesticide in her placenta – it can be as many as 17.

We have to reinvent the modern world so that it is compatible with nature's circular pattern of life and death and new growth. The concept of sustainability is all we have to set us on a new course.

Aftermath of the 2004 tsunami, Sri Lanka
© Arko Datta/Reuters

Five times in the past half-billion years, the fossil record shows us, living things have been wiped out over much of the earth.

Climate change, perhaps triggered by the impact of an asteroid, is the likely cause of the five great natural extinctions that geologists have identified. These acts of nature, like the 2004 tsunami that ravaged much of Southeast Asia, are part of the cycle of life and death that has defined the planet since the beginning of time. This haunting picture by Arko Datta of Indira Mariyappam mourning a relative brings home the horror of this natural tragedy.

We now face the sixth great extinction, and it will be an entirely human achievement. The combined effects of climate change, acidification of the seas as they soak up atmospheric CO_2 from our smoke stacks and exhaust pipes, the widespread destruction of forests, wetlands and other natural habitats, are together causing the loss of an estimated 50,000 species a year – an unseen holocaust of biodiversity.

Voodoo ceremony, Haiti

This photograph provides a glimpse of a secret world behind a closed door. A life dependent on the seasons unfolding in harmony with agricultural needs creates a culture steeped in superstition and fear.

I had become friends with the witch doctor in this remote part of Haiti, and he invited me along. He told me the rains had not come to the village for two years. "The soil is blowing away – and so are the young people. When they've gone they never come back."

Ask yourself, as you watch these people reach to their gods in a crisis, if we are acting rationally, logically, in the face of our problems. Are we able to question our values and see if they are appropriate for the conditions we now confront?

Feeding centre, Ethiopia, 1986
© Chris Steele-Perkins/Magnum

A moment in the off-and-on drought that killed hundreds of thousands in the 1970s and 80s in the Sahel region of Africa, leading to the Band Aid movement. Now we learn that the drought may have been caused by Western air pollution from cars and power stations. Burning coal and oil produces tiny airborne particles of soot, ash and sulphur compounds as well as invisible CO_2. These particles may displace rainfall as far away as Africa and Asia. This example of the catastrophic effects of human pollution on people who had no hand in causing it shows that, without a planetary policy on climate change and pollution, the prospects for new kinds of human strife are immense.

Either we learn to cooperate and live without polluting the earth or we must harden our hearts to the sound of children and their parents dying from man-made catastrophes.

To quote David Skitt once again:

"The tribal-national model, brought about by our genes as an appropriate means of survival in the environment of past millennia, is hopelessly inadequate as an adaptation to the present planetary challenges. However, we are nonetheless able, as the evolutionary biologist Richard Dawkins puts it, 'to rebel against our genes', and he has called this 'an unexpected bonus' at our present point in history. It is quite clearly now impossible to defend our national interests without simultaneously taking into account the interests of other nations and of the planet as a whole. This is an inescapable fact and a wholly new way of looking at the world and our position in it. Put another way, unless xenophobia gives way to species loyalty – a deeply felt sense of all of us being in the same boat – we are very unlikely to achieve unprecedented international cooperation and are more likely to have unprecedented conflict due to outmoded economic, political and religious divisions."

Central Park, New York, USA

One-fifth of the world's population lives in the "rich world". We consume 86% of the world's goods but most of us are not happy. Money buys a better quality of misery, a condition sometimes called affluenza, an epidemic of stress, overwork, waste and indebtedness caused by the pursuit of the American dream. Those of us who use the earth's resources at the rate of three or even five planets would do well to ask ourselves if we can live better with less.

Mother and child living in a drainpipe, Calcutta, India

Almost half the people on earth (nearly three billion) try to exist on the equivalent of less than $2 a day. The absolute poor try to exist on the equivalent of $1 a day. There are 1.1 billion of these people. They cannot meet their basic needs – food, clean water, shelter – and by definition not meeting basic needs often leads to premature death. Their children tend to die in large numbers – about 1.7 million every year due to old illnesses like diarrhoea and sleeping sickness. Their rain is now.
Lloyd Timberlake

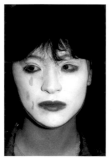

Carnival, Copenhagen, Denmark

Many of us in the modern world have felt a sense of loss, of missing something, in spite of our great technological gains, which should have made us feel that life has been enriched rather than impoverished. This crisis is constantly sustained and exacerbated by a basic and pervasive disharmony between the intellect and emotions that has been increasing since very early times. This disharmony is mirrored in our personal relationships, in relationships between governments, and in our relationship with nature.

Indeed, for both the rich and poor, life is dominated by an ever-growing current of problems, most of which seem to have no real and lasting solution. Clearly, we have not touched the deeper causes of our troubles. The ultimate source of all these problems is in thought itself, the very thing of which our civilization is most proud, and therefore the one thing that is "hidden" because of our failure seriously to engage with its actual working in our own individual lives and in the life of society.
David Bohm, Changing Consciousness

Drought, Namibia
© Mark Hakansson/Panos Pictures

A San Bushman boy stays beside his horse dying of thirst.

The world we were born into no longer exists; it's slipping away. More extreme weather events are recorded all over the world as the earth heats up: unprecedented heat waves in India, Pakistan, Bangladesh, Europe and North America, record melting of ice in the Arctic Ocean, and a record incidence of tropical storms. Shortly before being swept out of office, the Australian

Prime Minister John Howard, one of the last climate-change doubters, appealed to his countrymen to pray for rain to end a six-year super-drought, the first glimpse of climate change ravaging a developed nation.

These early warnings signal the massive disruption we will all face if we continue to pump greenhouse gases into the atmosphere. Prayers and voodoo ceremonies are not the answer; we need new leaders: men and women who see the real threats behind complex problems and can explain these to people, build coalitions and lay out solutions.

Abu Ghraib prison, Iraq, 2004
Photographer unknown

Suspected terrorists were tortured in secret prisons in at least eight countries during the Bush years. The now discredited practices ranged from waterboarding to collaring prisoners before slamming them naked against a wall. This photograph and the memos sanctioning torture by top officers in the Bush administration are sickening reminders of how short a journey we have taken towards a fair society and how quickly the structures that hold governments to justice can be eroded.

I gave a copy of Hard Rain to Al Gore. He opened the book and started singing Dylan's song, interrupting himself with comments as he turned the pages: "I've always thought this was one of the greatest lyrics written in my life – I still sing it to my kids." When he came to "I met a white man who walked a black dog", tears filled his eyes and he stopped. The environment movement benefited from Gore's losing the election but here was proof that America would have had a great president if the majority vote had counted in 2000.

Woman dying of AIDS, Ethiopia

To witness the HIV/AIDS epidemic is like watching a war film with the sound switched off. So much death taking place alone and in silence because AIDS is considered a shameful disease. These two women in Addis Ababa are part of a rota: HIV-positive women who are well take care of those who are dying.

They invited me to a meeting. Everyone was HIV-positive. A young woman asked how she could tell her children that she didn't have long to live. Another person – she seemed to overflow with affection – said, "Oh, make your children a meal, a wonderful meal with all the things they love. Make it lovingly and sit with them and then tell them that you can't be their mother for much longer but you will love them for ever."

The drugs to make AIDS a chronic illness, instead of a killer disease, have been available in the West for over a decade.

After a long, inexcusable delay, antiretroviral treatments are reaching some HIV-positive people in the developing world. Too late for these women who had to find the courage to say goodbye to their children.

My god-daughter Alice Jacoby in mid-air, catching rainbows in a teapot, England

While children play, we grown-ups contribute $1 trillion a year to the world's military budget to protect ourselves from other grown-ups just like us. How do we divert some of this bloated budget to secure the future so that children alive now won't suffer the consequences of our wasteful, polluting way of living?

Reinventing the world so that it is sustainable will require a huge investment. We have the money; the problem is that it is being spent on weapons of mass destruction. If we could only trust each other somewhat, we could divert part of that military budget to building a secure world.

Child burial, Taj Mahal, India

This child died an unnecessary death from an illness that could have been treated with a few pills we in the West would buy from a chemist. He is buried next to his sister, who died the day before him in the shadow of the Taj Mahal.

Children are the welfare state in developing countries. People choose to have smaller families when they are confident that their children will survive to take care of them in old age. As communities and countries develop, as child healthcare is made available, as women are educated and have the chance of employment, population growth falls. Poverty and population expansion are inextricably linked.

Shattered graveyard portrait of a dead Palestinian, Lebanon
© Chris Steele-Perkins/Magnum

The boundaries between nations are created entirely by thinking. As you cross the boundary there is no physical change, and very often the people are not all that different. The difference is entirely due to differences in custom and habit and history that began by their thinking differently. They gradually came to have different languages and to have somewhat different ways of life… And yet people are supposed to die for nations, and give up all their possessions for them, and put their children in the army for them, and sacrifice everything for them.
David Bohm, Changing Consciousness

Canaima National Park, Venezuela
© David Woodfall/Still Pictures

Perhaps the single most important thing that we can do to undo the harm we have done is to fix firmly in our minds the thought: the earth is alive. Once such a thought becomes instinctive we would know that we cannot cut down forests for farmland to feed ourselves without risking the destruction of our home planet. Farmland and tree plantations cannot serve as a replacement for natural forests that have evolved with their environment over millions of years and once served to keep the climate tolerable and the air good to breathe.
James Lovelock, Earthy Realism

Lovelock developed the Gaia theory in which he proposed that living and non-living parts of the earth are a complex interacting system that can be thought of as a single organism. According to the theory, all living things have a regulatory, life-promoting effect on the earth's environment. Gaia theory brings together a science-based idea in tune with the wisdom of our ancestors and challenges the mechanistic Newtonian view that allows us to behave like asset-stripping owners of the earth.

Logging road, Amazon, Brazil

Surui children watch a bulldozer cut a logging road through their reservation. This picture records the moment when indigenous wisdom and a foreign photographer are humiliated by the modern world. The parents of these children were forced to sell timber to pay for medicines to treat TB. They were infected when the infamous BR364 highway was built through their land. Their medicine men, like our scientists, cannot suddenly develop cures for new diseases. So now their culture is drawn into scientific civilization. One more perplexing example of indigenous people, shorn of their ancient cultures, walking into the darkness of an unknown future – their rituals, artefacts and wisdom diminished for ever by the devastating effectiveness of science.

Just before I took this picture, I got in the way of the bulldozer and a tree fell on top of me. I was trapped, miraculously unhurt, between two forked branches. A distant memory of Laurel and Hardy came to mind as I pulled myself out of the tree. They are arguing about the best way to build a house when it falls on them. Standing in line with an open window, they don't notice their home in pieces all around them.

I hope that isn't an unfortunate analogy. Our politicians have to prove Elliot Richardson wrong: "Environmentalists and politicians can argue the costs and benefits of international action on global warming from now until doomsday, and they probably will."

Serra Pelada gold mine, Amazon
© Sebastião Salgado/NB Pictures

Thousands of dust-covered labourers swarm over this mine site deep in the Amazon, a tropical version of the 19th-century Klondike: the poorest people mining the most desirable metal. It will end up in bank vaults, as jewellery, coins, and fillings in our teeth. And few who use it will have an idea of the human and environmental cost of extracting it from the crust of the earth.

Child workers, Manila Bay, Philippines
© Hartmut Schwarzbach/UNEP/Still Pictures

The unacceptable face of recycling. These children collect plastic from the polluted waters of Manila Bay to sort and sell to middlemen. They are among the 200 million working children around the world. Of those, 8.5 million are in slavery, a practice abolished 200 years ago.

La Paz, Bolivia

Our challenge, our generation's unique challenge, is learning to live peacefully and sustainably in an extraordinarily crowded world. Our planet is crowded to an unprecedented degree. It is bursting at the seams. It's bursting at the seams in human terms, in economic terms, and in ecological terms. This is our greatest challenge: learning to live in a crowded and interconnected world that is creating unprecedented pressures on human society and on the physical environment.
Jeffrey Sachs, 2007 Reith Lectures

Swimming with a humpback whale, French Polynesia
© Yves Lefèvre/BIOS/Still Pictures

The world of nature and the world of man are inter related. Man cannot escape from that. When he destroys nature, he is destroying himself. When he kills another, he is killing himself. The enemy is not the other but you. To live in such harmony with nature, with the world, naturally brings about a different world.
J. Krishnamurti, Letters to the Schools, Vol. 2

Kosovan refugees
© J. Dago/UNEP/Still Pictures

Bread is thrown to Kosovan refugees prevented from re-entering the former Yugoslav Republic of Macedonia.

"We are in conflict with each other, and our world is being destroyed. There is crisis after crisis, war after war: there is starvation, misery; there are the enormously rich, clothed in their respectability, and there are the poor. To solve these problems, what is necessary is not a new system of thought, not a new economic revolution, but to understand what is – the discontent, the constant probing of what is – which will bring about a revolution which is more far-reaching than the revolution of ideas. And it is this revolution that is so necessary to bring about a different culture, a different religion, a different relationship between man and man."
J. Krishnamurti, Reflections on the Self

The Andromeda Galaxy
© O. Sauzereau/BIOS/Still Pictures

The universe was still the size of your living room until the big telescopes came along. Now we have an idea of just how fragile and isolated our situation really is… When all this kicks in, this information that's only sixty or seventy years old, we'll have a very different view of our place and purpose here. And all this rat-race, turf-war, dog-eat-dog stuff we do all day will be revealed for what it is. The revolution is coming… And it's a revolution of consciousness.
Martin Amis, Night Train

A wedding party protests against air pollution, Russia
© A. Zhdanov/UNEP/Still Pictures

We all have to put huge pressure on our governments to introduce the policy changes that are required to solve the climate crisis and related environmental and social problems.

Write letters to city, state, county, provincial and national governments; to United Nations agencies and the World Bank; to companies large and small; to churches, mosques and synagogues. If you are one of the five billion people who belong to the faith communities around the world, join the campaign for a sustainable future on earth.

Jacabamba valley, Peru
© Bryan and Mark Lynas/Still Pictures

It was with some trepidation that I trekked up Jacabamba valley, following in my father's footsteps some twenty years before. From a distance the snow-capped peaks looked the same as in his photos, but the real question I wanted to answer was what the big fan-shaped glacier above the lake looked like today. I reached the spot in a little over three hours, rounding a hill of glacial moraine to arrive at the lake. It was barely recognizable, and for a minute I thought there must have been some mistake. The big fan-shaped glacier had vanished, leaving in its place bare rock and a few heaps of grey rubble.

Lima is the second-largest desert city in the world after Cairo, and every drop of water consumed by its seven million residents flows down from the Andes high above. Much of the dry-season flow of the coastal rivers is sustained by glacier melt, and if these glaciers disappear then the rivers will run dry for half the year. The process is already well under way: in the past thirty years 811 million cubic metres of water (three times the volume of Windermere, England's largest lake) has been lost from the ice-fields above Lima. It's a problem mirrored in the Indian subcontinent, where some estimates suggest that half a billion people will run short of water over the next century as the Himalayan glaciers retreat.
Mark Lynas

Inuit hunter, Baffin Island, Canada
© Gordon Wiltsie/Peter Arnold Inc/
Still Pictures

A hundred years from now, half the world's climates may have vanished because of global warming. Gone too will be the traditional ways of life of indigenous people who depend on extensive, intact wilderness.

Crying to the spirits: a portrait of a Hidatsa man, USA, 1908
© Edward S. Curtis

The Hidatsa people lived along the Missouri from Heart River to the Little Missouri in North Dakota. According to legend, their emergence was a mythical one from the underworld.

This photograph is by one of the world's greatest photographers, Edward S. Curtis. In 1898, at the age of 30, he had the idea to photograph all aspects of a marvellous culture being inexorably destroyed. He wanted to make more than just a record of North American Indian life. His ambition was to retain the spirit of their culture and keep it alive.

But photographs can't keep cultures alive. Curtis's magnificent pictures of dignified people tell us something we all know but forget too easily: that to keep our cultures alive we have to question our values and see if they are appropriate for the conditions we face. Success or failure depends on which values we hold on to and which we discard and replace with new ones when times change.

THE ECOLOGY OF PAIN

Tim Smit

Tim Smit is Chief Executive and co-founder of the Eden Project in Cornwall, a once sterile clay pit transformed into a cradle of life combining world-class horticulture with architecture and installations celebrating the application of science, human endeavour and sustainable living. Tim is also Director of the nearby Lost Gardens of Heligan, which he restored with John Nelson.

Born in Holland and educated in Britain, after working as an archaeologist for two years, he switched to the music business and spent ten years as a composer and producer. Tim is a trustee, patron and board member of a wide range of statutory and voluntary bodies, and a member of the Council on Social Action, advising the UK government and other key stakeholders on ideas and initiatives to inspire, facilitate and celebrate social change. He was awarded an Honorary CBE in 2002.

www.edenproject.com
www.heligan.com

I am extremely proud of the Eden Project's association with Mark Edwards. When he first suggested the idea for Hard Rain as a photographic essay resetting the Cold War anti-nuclear lyric of Bob Dylan's song to fit our changing times, we were immediately excited by it. The lyric would tell a different story, one no less terrifying in anticipation, but here hardened with a wider narrative that shames our claim to the title *Homo sapiens*.

The first exhibition was launched at Eden in May 2006 and it stayed up for nine months. Nearly a million people saw it and were moved. We have never had such a postbag for an exhibition, nor such expressions of outrage and admiration. Why? People must surely watch the TV news, or read newspapers? They couldn't be shocked or surprised, could they? Well, many agreed that they were aware of the individual tragedies or situations illustrated in the photographs, but what got to them emotionally was the combination of poetry (as opposed to commentary) and the harsh beauty of the imagery, which in turn made them complicit.

Each person reacts differently to being confronted by images as compelling as those of Hard Rain. Some can view them with near-detachment, reading them as an allegory, a cautionary tale. Moving, as a great work of art is moving, but not *experienced*. Others see them as a call to action, an incitement to impotent rage, or as evidence for the eternal failings of mankind and a reason for depression or cynical despair. However, a connection was made and connection is the most important thing.

We live in a communication age, yet the distinction between transmission and reception is lost on most communicators, who seem content to address each other. As any fascist will tell you, uplifting exhortations and the big picture can stir the heart to action and create a momentum behind an agenda that is played as serving those ends, but if you don't have a vision of the future, a narrative that leads you to the sunlit uplands of the imagination, that hints at a future possible with you, yes you, as a player in the story, it will perish on the vine. As the great anthropologist and myth collector Joseph Turnbull has said, the purpose of myth is to create meaning, not describe fact.

Those who believe that societies with a rich mythology are "primitive" are blind to their own. Why is it that we now go to a supermarket not to buy eggs, but to buy eggs that have come from chickens free to eat where they like? Some of them are organic and the boxes in which the eggs are contained are biodegradable. What is this if it is not the start of a journey towards meaning, towards reconnection with nature? This and the myriad other stories growing up around the way we live and consume are the first stirrings of a society rediscovering its need to belong to and be a part of nature, not apart from it.

C.S. Lewis once said, "While science may lead you to truth, only the imagination can lead you to meaning." It is arguable that the near-messianic way we have begun to embrace climate change, and the need to address our behaviour by bringing it more in tune with "natural" ways of living, are part of a fundamental shift in a global culture instinctively ill at ease with its direction. Climate change is both a real threat and a symbol of "the Fall", reigniting a secular thirst for spiritual transformation and belonging which will see our national narratives embrace concepts of community and responsibility with a fervour previously reserved for the cult of the individual. All across Europe and in the United States fertile ground is being prepared for this.

Charles Darwin's world-changing and culture-shaping concept of natural selection, the idea of the survival of the fittest (meant by Darwin to reflect "fit for purpose", as in having adaptations to an environment giving the best chance of survival), has strangely been understood by many to see evolution as a form of design development that will relentlessly lead to "perfection" – a super-adapted life form.

In Dan Quinn's wonderful book *Ishmael* a man answers a newspaper advertisement seeking a pupil who sincerely wants to change the world. The teacher turns out to be a talking gorilla (the reason for which is convincingly explained) who asks the man a question as a condition of agreeing to teach him: "What is the myth that all humans live by?" Unable to find a universal myth he begs his teacher for a clue, whereupon he has his moment of revelation. The myth we live by is so big we miss it: that the whole purpose of evolution was to arrive at Homo sapiens – life perfected. When finally the man concedes that every single law of nature applies as much to man as to any other living thing, the gorilla asks a simple question: "Why then do you not in your universities study whether there are natural laws pertaining to the ways in which animals live together, for the lesson is that if there are, they will surely apply to man?"

The present is never a good place to imagine the future. We know two things for certain about it: first, that the background noise of our personal lives and the needs of the now will distract us; second, the future as imagined will always be wrong. While the science-fiction writers of the 1950s imagined almost every technical invention that we now take for granted, hardly anyone, with the possible exception of Aldous Huxley, imagined the massive social change that would transform society over the next fifty years. Emerging gender equality, ethnic diversity, human rights, gay rights, single families, the ageing population and the transformation of ideas about what constitutes a nuclear family were almost entirely missed.

It is important to acknowledge that over the last twenty or so years there has been a huge improvement in living conditions all over the world. The fact that there remains such an unimaginable number of people in poverty, without access to basic needs, or to the minimum of human rights, is a disgrace when measured against our publicly stated aspirations for the improvement of the human condition. But as an absolute things have got better and continue to do so (according to some criteria). What is extraordinary is that the number of people moving out of poverty is huge, but in percentage terms it remains virtually the same as it was in 1909 and 1959. Is there a mechanism missing to unlock the development agenda further still?

The success of new business models such as the micro-credit revolution inspired by Muhammad Yunus's Grameen Bank, first in Bangladesh, but now extending into many other countries, appears to point a way towards liberation from poverty and hence returning control of people's destinies to themselves and their communities.

There is much evidence that wealth generation and education lead to a decline in birth rates; poverty alleviation lies at the heart of any solution to population control. The fact that with increasing wealth come other demands, including dietary change, which in turn has implications for land use and food security, is a distinct issue needing different approaches. An example would be organizations such as Slum Dwellers International (SDI), whose philosophy and operating strategy encourage the creation of groups or associations of the poor which make themselves "visible" both to themselves and to government institutions. While undoubtedly many of the participants have found it difficult coming to terms with being a member of such a new construct, the impact on their wellbeing and ability to influence political and economic systems to their advantage is reshaping the landscape for the poor.

The environmentalist Paul Hawken in his recent book *Blessed Unrest* describes the new emerging politics of NGOs and pressure groups, estimating that globally there exist nearly a million such organizations. Hawken takes a very optimistic slant on this vast yet leaderless group of interests and likens them to the antibodies in the human immune system, getting together to fight an infection and then moving on. He sees this as the emergence of a movement that is totally new and moreover one that has a tool at its disposal that was previously unavailable: the internet. The speed of communication and the availability of open-source knowledge is an exhilarating development and one that redefines many things, including our ideas about what constitutes a culture.

Beyond this we see the emerging role of the virtual societies that are springing up on the web – the Facebook generation. I was in a meeting with one of the directors of Cisco Systems, who said: "Up until two years ago, maybe, all our new graduate intakes were focused on wealth creation and a simple philosophy that went along the lines of 'knowledge is power'. However, since then, as new graduates have come in, their take on it is that knowledge is to be shared – it is part of their DNA. It has already changed the way we are looking at the future."

I would date the roots of this new generation to the Horn of Africa famine of 1984–5 where millions were displaced and over a million died. The pictures made harrowing watching, and although compassion fatigue inevitably set in, every time an individual story was highlighted the strong reactions returned. When someone is there in front of us with a name and a story to tell – we respond. Despite the cynicism that often sets in post-event, Live Aid was a seminal moment in making a huge number of people realize the enormous power that connectivity could unleash. It painted a prospect of a better world where a light shone into the dark corners. Nearly thirty years later this vision is coming to pass.

What is it that silences the voices of idealism? Does the righteous anger of youth get deflected by the first flush of adulthood and the attendant responsibilities of the hamster's embrace of the treadmill? At what point do we come over all reasonable and realistic – the faux adult position that the world is more complicated than our youthful naïvety suggested? Crusading journalists such as John Pilger, Noam Chomsky or Edward Said are lauded for their bravery and insight, yet the background noise of other more "realistic" observers paints them into a corner where they are defined as "other", slightly embarrassing. Worse yet is the implication that one has fallen for a conspiracy theory. Ah, the conspiracy theory, the secret weapon of all great conspirators…

When you see a child in flames, a husband cradling his poisoned wife, dogs eating a corpse or a man in a wasteland cutting the last remaining tree, is there anyone with humanity that would not have wished it otherwise? A palette of pain and suffering is relatively easy to marshal, and to add to the woes with a further litany is overkill. Edward Said, who first described the need to create "otherness" to help the self-definition of those who were doing the describing and hence feeding the demonization or victimization of others, would enjoy seeing the weaponry turned to advantage by the dispossessed. Who would have thought that a quiet man with a great vision, Muhammad Yunus, could have reinvented corporate action in a highly successful business venture that has the poor as the main stakeholders? Who would have believed that young people pouring out of our universities could have turned the concept of "knowledge is power" on its head and sought to make knowledge freely available to all? Who would have believed that the excesses of Wall Street would have been condemned as selfish, greedy and ultimately damaging to everything most of us believe in, by none other than the President of the United States? And what of those old gurus Milton Friedman, Hayek et al., with their vision of a dog-eat-dog world where wealth would trickle down like crumbs from the rich man's table? They would have us believe that we are better off because of their work and their belief in the free market rampant and the myth they peddled of a world where growth could continue into the infinite future. We are brighter than that, we are Hom. sap... how could we believe it? Dan Quinn's gorilla could just as easily have had this as the myth that all men live by.

Jared Diamond in his book *Collapse* writes about the rise and fall of civilizations from the beginning of recorded time. The inevitability of collapse is extraordinary. The causes of it are not; almost all societies have collapsed because of the vanity of their rulers. The urge to build bigger monuments, have a bigger population and run out of natural resources to support this is a theme that runs through them all. The Anastazi, the Maya, the Sumerians, the Assyrians, the Babylonians, Egyptians, Greeks, Romans, the Easter Islanders: each pushed the limits of nature beyond balance and paid the price. Interestingly, there are only two societies that have stood the test of time and who have remained uninfected for more than three thousand years. They are the Papua New Guinea Highlanders and the people of Tikopia, a tiny island in Melanesia. What have they got in common? They both created social structures and rules which set limits to growth and protected their environment. The Tikopians went so far as to forego having pigs on their island despite pig owning being a sign of wealth and power. They realized that the island couldn't sustain it and in an act of extraordinary solidarity killed all pigs allowing no exceptions.

The Sumerians invented accountancy, which in turn developed writing (initially as lists for accountants). The ordering of things by number and the mathematics of accumulation, which in turn would lead to new power structures that would centralize control, has been practised by each of the civilizations that has turned to dust. We know, with hindsight, that democracy only occurs where more than one group, preferably many, own rights or have access to resources without which the others cannot exercise control. There is no example of a true democracy where there are not many stakeholders. Imposing one where this isn't the case has always resulted in failure. We have seen that stakeholding can be achieved through the artificial construct of new social groupings (SDI), we have seen where economic strength can be generated by empowering the poor (Grameen) and we have seen the power of public opinion released through "open source" access to knowledge, and, in Hawken, the emergence of a leaderless group of organizations and agencies acting as if they were antibodies to the body politic.

Hindsight would confirm all these things to be true. Yet we are in the present reflecting on the future, and history teaches us that writers always get this wrong. Returning to Dan Quinn's gorilla and his question about natural laws, almost every government and corporation in the world is run on a mechanistic accountancy-based model as if there was a Copernican *deus ex machina* at play, yet our private lives do not conform to these rigid hierarchies and structures and nowhere in nature is this to be found. Hawken's observations about the ebb and flow of the NGOs and pressure groups ring true, as does the observation about the emerging virtual society. They have a biological imperative at their heart, not a mechanistic one. The Grameen Bank's success is based on humane values and rules of engagement. They are intensely personal. All these examples hint at something very significant going on.

My father-in-law once said something that has stuck with me: all the problems in the world, save accidents of health or natural disaster, are solvable by common courtesy. Hard Rain is a searing vision of a world in which so much is wrong, and it would be easy to see it through world-weary eyes. Yes, the list of iniquities seems endless, the cruelties and greed of men appear to be unstoppable, yet do stop and ponder the new narrative emerging. Do you not feel the call of destiny, the stirrings of hope that we might just be living in times when we can imagine people like us, all over the world, each drawing confidence from the other? Lighting a bonfire in our hearts to remember to be angry once again and restate our belief in the human values that all religions have tried to harness to themselves – but with such a spectacular failure to deliver that it should now be the turn of the humane secularists? I said earlier that Aldous Huxley was perhaps the only writer who came close to imagining our social future, but I prefer that his vision of a Brave New World is turned into a humane New Brave World, one that reflects our transformation to a narrative based on living with the grain of nature and away from a desire to control all aspects of it – something that hindsight tells us has always resulted in failure.

Hard Rain holds a mirror up to the many faces of pain. Relief, if there is any, comes in knowing deep inside what we could be and the shame at how far we still have to go to evolve to a place our imagination tells us we can reach. A smart observer once remarked, "It's not the disappointment that kills you, it's the hope." Dame Barbara Ward, the founder of IIED, said, "We all have a duty to hope", meaning we have a duty to keep hope alive and act on its possibilities, and she was right. The irony of course is that Bob Dylan's lyric, like the social futurologists of the 50s, was wrong. I hope that his lyric, newly set to Mark Edwards' photographs, can be proved wrong all over again. That way hope lies.

CHANGING CONSCIOUSNESS

David Bohm

A consistent theme throughout Hard Rain is the need for a new spirit of cooperation if we are to solve the problems we face.

This chapter explores the hidden obstacles to cooperation. It's an extract from a book Professor David Bohm and I collaborated on, snappily titled *Changing Consciousness: Exploring the Hidden Source of the Social, Political, and Environmental Crises Facing our World*. It was published in 1989 by Harper San Francisco.

David Bohm was a brilliant theoretical physicist – Einstein called him his intellectual successor – and one of the most original thinkers of the second half of the 20th century. In 1959 his wife Saral came across a book by the modern philosopher and educator J. Krishnamurti and suggested he read it. They were in a public library and he didn't put it down until he had finished it. He was impressed by the way the philosophical ideas expressed in *Freedom from the Known* meshed with his own ideas on quantum mechanics. David went on to meet Krishnamurti and to work closely with him in a collaboration that lasted many years.

For David this meeting made possible the insight that a "wrong functioning of thought" is behind most of the troubles in the human race. This insight went along with an understanding of the need for a certain kind of observation of how thought is actually working, whether one is thinking independently or merely taking part in the activities of society.

I came across Krishnamurti while I was at art school in 1966. The key effect for me was to arouse an intense curiosity to see with my own eyes how the development of civilization has had a wide range of negative consequences, not only in society and in the natural environment, but also in the culture and general health of the mind. I have tried to convey in pictures the destructive effects of the disorder in thought to which Krishnamurti had so passionately called attention.

The course of both our lives was deeply changed by this contact with Krishnamurti, who introduced us in 1983 at Brockwood Park School. David and Saral had played a key role in helping establish the school, which was founded by Krishnamurti in 1969.

By this time I had already spent many years photographing people living at the sharp end of the environmental debate. I wanted to explore David's ideas in relation to the problems I was witnessing. The project held more than a professional interest for me. It is difficult to enter the world of the poor; it's a world you never entirely leave.

I was disturbed by the scale of people's suffering, particularly in the majority world but also closer to home. Everywhere I looked, problems overwhelmed solutions and solutions turned into more complex problems.

Working with David proved to be an extraordinary education. It is hoped that this chapter will introduce David's ideas to a new readership and will open up further lines of inquiry that could perhaps lead to an understanding of the deeper causes of our troubles at this critical time in our history.
Mark Edwards

David Bohm: Every nation has come into existence through some thought that said, "We exist; we declare that we exist, we have our independence", or else it gradually came to that. Thus, we now have a lot of nations that never existed before – a hundred years ago the world map was utterly different. And yet people are supposed to die for nations, and give up all their possessions for them, and put their children into the army for them and sacrifice everything for them. People forget that the boundaries between nations are created entirely by thinking. As you cross the boundary there is no physical change, and very often the people are not all that different. The difference is entirely due to differences in custom and habit and history that began by their thinking differently. They gradually came to have different languages and to have somewhat different ways of life. Then they said, "Here we have a nation," and they thought, "We're all united within our nation – we're different from all other nations."

Of course, nations may serve a useful purpose as convenient administrative units, and these may correspond to groups of people with a fairly common culture as well as other common interests. But the importance of the differences between nations has always been enormously exaggerated. Indeed, different nations are fairly closely connected physically, and now in the modern world the connection is much closer. Economically we all depend on one another, and ecologically we're seeing that, with the change of climate and for other reasons, we will all suffer together when things go wrong. So there are a great many key points at which we are intimately bound together. The idea of national sovereignty denies this and says that each nation can do what it likes. This would only make sense if the

nations really were independent of each other. But people are overlooking our interdependence and saying that no one can tell our nation what to do. Yet, for example, in Brazil they are cutting down and burning the rainforests. Some of the Brazilian politicians are saying with resentment that you northern, prosperous people are producing most of the carbon dioxide and you are then blaming us for changing the climate. Who do you think you are to tell us what to do with our Amazon? And we in the north similarly say, who do you in Brazil think you are to tell us what to do with our industries? But talking this way, how can we ever get together to stop all this destructive activity?

This way of thinking has been given a name: fragmentation. The word *fragment* means to smash, to break up. It doesn't mean to divide. The parts of a watch could be divided, but they could still make up the whole. However, if you smashed the watch, you would get fragments, parts just arbitrarily broken up. People tend to think of nations as parts, but they are really fragments. If you try to take out one nation from the whole context, trade and all sorts of other connections would be broken. Moreover, people pretend that their nation is more united than it actually is. There are all sorts of divisions within each nation that are often far worse than those between nations.

Fragmentation consists of false division, making a division where there is a tight connection, and also false unification, uniting where there is not unity. For example, I say there is no nation that is really united. There is tremendous conflict within each nation – between the poor and the rich, between the bureaucracy and the people, between one ethnic group and another. So it is a fiction that any nation is united and that one nation is sharply distinct from another. And evidently, if we try to live by fiction, we are going to get into trouble. So it is this fragmentation, this fictional way of thinking, that has created all this trouble and produced the armies and the nuclear bombs and the refugees with all their suffering and also our inability to solve the ecological problems, and economic problems, and so on.

Mark Edwards: I think it is difficult to see that thought can create what appear to be independently real things, things like these divisions. Thought tends to assume that it is only reflecting what is actually there, not producing what is there.

DB: Yes. Of course, there is a kind of thought that is more or less a representation of what is there, like a map. However, thought has a creative function as well, to create what is there. In fact, almost everything we see around us in the world was created from thought, including all the cities, all the buildings, all the science, all the technology, and almost everything that we call nature. Farmland was produced by thought, by people thinking what they're going to do with the land and then doing it. So without thought we wouldn't have farms; we wouldn't have factories; we wouldn't have ships; we wouldn't have airplanes; we wouldn't have governments. Supposing we have a company like General Motors. People have to think to know what they are supposed to be doing – if they all forgot this, the company would collapse and would cease to exist. So thought can take part in creativity. Thought has created a lot of good things. It is a very powerful instrument, but if we don't notice how it works, it can also do great harm.

ME: Some in the environmental movement are pointing out that nationalism makes it very difficult to solve the world's environmental problems. And they feel that nationalism in some magical way will lose its hold on people. I can't see that happening without a sustained inquiry into the process of thought that has produced nationalism – in fact, the reverse seems more likely, especially if conditions get worse along lines that are predicted.

DB: What we must do first is understand the source, otherwise what one says about ending nationalism may be just a vain hope. People in the Middle Ages hoped that the plague would go away, but they didn't realize that it was carried by fleas, which in turn were carried by rats, which were carried by ships from one country to another. They didn't think about the fleas and the rats and the ships. Later people saw the rats coming out of the ships, and they knew they were carrying fleas and realized the connection between fleas and plague and on the ropes holding the ships they built plates so that rats couldn't come ashore. That was a big step in stopping the plague, because they'd learned how it was carried. So if nationalism is the plague, we have to understand the origin of that plague.

To meet this challenge, we have to begin by examining the general nature of thought. To begin with, we can say that thought is knowledge that is being applied to a particular case or that is being created by thinking about things. You begin to think, "What shall I do? What's this all about?" What you think then goes into the memory; it becomes a kind of program. In thinking something, it becomes thought – the language says so. The word *thinking* means something active is going on; the word *thought* means it has gone on. You usually think that thought has gone and therefore has no effect. But thought has actually gone into the program, into the memory. It's not really just the memory of what has happened, but also of what to do, of what to believe, of how things should be divided up or united, of who you are, of what you belong to, and all that. Now, when this memory works, it doesn't come back as thinking; it works almost immediately, without thinking, through the way you respond, through its effect on how you see things, and so on.

Young children never know that one nation is different from another until they're told. But when they're told by people whom they believe – their parents or whoever it is – they think, "Well, now we know." And when they know, they don't have to think anymore. It is thought that now works and, for example, makes them feel uneasy with a foreign person. Thought affects the body, creating the stance of being cautious. And the adrenaline flows, because there is a certain amount of fear and mistrust, not quite the sense of ease you have with someone you know. Thought works in this way for all sorts of things. If you want to drive a car, you have to be told all sorts of things; you have to learn how. But when you drive, you act without thinking. If you had to think before applying what you've learned, it would be too late. The same kind of thought that enables you to drive a car operates when you become hostile to someone of another group, whether it be a different race, nation, or religion.

Suppose you have two religions. Thought defines religion – the thought about the nature of God and various questions like that. Such thought is very important because it is about God, who is supposed to be supreme. The thought about what is of supreme value must have the highest

force. So if you disagree about that, the emotional impact can be very great, and you will then have no way to settle it. Two different beliefs about God will thus produce intense fragmentation – similarly with thoughts about the nature of society, which is also very important, or with ideologies such as communism and capitalism, or with different beliefs about your family or about your money. Whatever it is that is very important to you, fragmentation in your thought about it is going to be very powerful in its effects.

ME: Yes, and politicians are particularly adroit at manipulating this tendency to fragmentary thinking in the form of nationalism. In fact, their careers depend on it.

DB: Well, they think about it all the time, and it's now in their thought. People accept it as a matter of course that they can't trust people in another country. And when they think about it, they see that equally one can't trust the people in their own country. Fundamentally the people in one's own country are no more trustworthy than they are anywhere else – every politician knows that.

ME: There are some divisions that appear to be more real than national boundaries – the Asiatic world, with its religious traditions, and the industrialized world, with its materialistic traditions emphasizing technology. However, in the long run, the differences may not be so great. The industrial world is poisoning the entire planet with chemical pollution, and in the Third World more and more land is being destroyed by deforestation and overpopulation caused mainly by poverty. I don't think that people are particularly happy or fulfilled in either culture. In the East people think that if they had our riches and security they'd be happy beyond measure; in the West we feel that we have lost something that they still have in the East. If we had a simpler life, closer to nature, we suppose, we would be at peace. (The rich have always romanticized poverty.) Can we examine this difference between the Asiatic world and the industrialized world in the light of what you have just said?

DB: First of all, this division arises out of the way people historically have thought differently in the Asiatic and the Western worlds. In the Western world thought has turned toward science and technology. Some historians, such as Joseph Needham, have asked why the Chinese didn't develop technology though they had a higher civilization than Europe had in the Middle Ages. He gave several explanations – we don't need to go into them in detail here. But for various reasons Western thought has turned toward technology and industrial development, perhaps partly because of its early emphasis on the concept of measure, which goes back to ancient Greece and even before. By contrast, partly because of the kind of philosophy that prevailed in the East, which put the immeasurable into first place, Eastern thought has been more static in its treatment of the domain of the measurable, and so people there have been more satisfied to stay with things as they are. But ultimately this difference is due to thought. It seems very unlikely that it is due to race; in many ways, the Japanese are doing better at certain key aspects of our Western thought than we are.

So there isn't any intrinsic distinction between Eastern and Western humanity that I can see operating. Differences exist because thought develops like a stream that happens to go one way here and another way there. Once it develops

it produces real physical results that people are looking at, but they don't see where these results are coming from – that's one of the basic features of fragmentation. When they have produced these divisions they see that real things have happened, so they'll start with these real things as if they just suddenly got there by themselves, or evolved in nature by themselves. That's the second mistake that thought makes.

It produces a result, and then it says, "I didn't do it; it's there by itself, and I must correct it." But if thought is constantly making this result and then saying, "I've got to stop it", this is absurd. Because thought is caught up in this absurdity, it is producing all sorts of negative consequences, then treating them as independent and saying, "I must stop them." It is as if man with his right hand were doing things he didn't want to do, and with the left hand he tried to hold back his right hand. All he has to do is to stop the whole process, and then he doesn't have that problem.

ME: What is it that would look at thought?

DB: This is a very subtle question. Let me begin by pointing out that the most fundamental characteristic of the word *thought* is that it is in the past tense. It is what has been thought, though it's still not gone. One of the common beliefs is that thought, when you've finished with it, has gone. But we've said that it is actually there, as if it were on the computer disk. The computer disk not only repeats all sorts of facts, but, even more important, it actually operates the computer in a certain way. That way has to be changed from time to time because things change. Or as Krishnamurti put it, thought and knowledge are limited. They cannot cover everything, if only because they are based on things that have happened in the past, whereas everything changes. However, one of the most common assumptions of thought is that thought is not limited.

ME: Most of us would see that thought is limited by experience and in its own way reflects experience.

DB: Thought is not just reflecting whatever is there, but on the basis of what is known from the past, it helps to create the impression of what is there. It selects; it abstracts; and in doing this, it chooses certain aspects, which then attract our attention. But what is there is immensely beyond what thought can grasp. As an analogy, consider a map: a map does not correspond with a territory in a direct and immediately perceptible way; it's only in some very abstract sense that it corresponds. For example, if you have a division between one country and another, there's a line on the map – that's an abstraction. And there's another line that is supposed to be somewhere in between the two countries – that's another abstraction. So there's a correspondence of these two abstractions. In this way, the map may enable you to see certain abstract relationships that could help guide you in the territory. But the map is much, much less than the territory, and it's not always even right. Thought could be regarded as a more abstract and generalized kind of map of reality.

ME: The difficulty here is to distinguish perception of the fact from the thought.

DB: That's right. That's one of the problems, that thought affects the way you see the fact and affects the way you see the territory. For example, when you cross from one country to another, you see another nation, but really, where is it? It's not there by itself; it's only there because you think it's there or because of what people have done because they think it's there. Therefore, thought is not keeping track of its own consequences, of its own activity. You need some sort of process of perception to keep track of that. You cannot by thinking alone look at the territory.

Thought is conditioned to react somewhat as if it were a computer disk and can therefore respond extremely rapidly. It is helpful to regard thought as acting basically like a conditioned reflex. It takes time to build up the memory-based reactions, but once this is done the responses are so fast that it is difficult to see their mechanical nature. For example, if you look at a tree, you'll immediately say the word *tree* rather as a disk on a computer set up to recognize the shape of a tree might do. All the information and general responses connected with this word are then called up automatically.

But reactive thought and perception of an actual fact are very different. The first point to notice is that we are able to perceive an actual fact through our senses. Everybody can see that we can perceive this through our senses, whether it be our eyes or our ears or our sense of touch, and that in this way we get information that thought cannot possibly supply. The least we can say, therefore, is that we have a combination of sense perception and thought.

I think that when this happens, we begin to go a bit beyond thought. Indeed, thought stops for a moment. In some sense we are then perceiving, but not through our senses; we are looking through the mind. Such perception, in which one goes deeply into the more subtle aspects of incoherence, can invalidate a false program so that subsequent thought can be free from it and therefore more coherent.

To sum up, then, thought is a response based on memory, but as one can discover by actual experience in the way that has just been described, it can be affected by perception, both through the senses and through the mind, and this is evidently not based primarily on memory. Through such perception, we can see the incoherence in our thought (for example, we can detect fragmentation). We can then go on to perceiving new ways of making distinctions and new relationships among the things thus distinguished that were more congruent with actual fact.

I suggest that this approach can be carried further to make possible new discoveries, new ideas, and new insights. All this indicates some faculty that goes beyond memory, that is not just sense perception. This is something we will explore in more detail later on, because it is of fundamental significance.

If I'm right in saying that thought is the ultimate origin or source, it follows that if we don't do anything about thought, we won't get anywhere. We may momentarily relieve the population problem, the ecological problem, and so on, but they will come back in another way. So I'm saying that we have got to examine the question of thought.

Now, how can you influence all these people? Well, you've got to begin with those who can listen, because everything new started with a few people. At the time of Newton, for example, there were not a hundred scientists of any merit in Europe. They could have said, "Look at this vast mass of ignorant people, going around just living their lives." Nevertheless, science had a tremendous effect, though not all to the good. But still, it shows that small things can have big effects – one small thing being, for example, more and more people understanding that something

has to change. We see the Green movement growing. They are doing good work, and much more should be done along these lines. But the important point is that they're not considering thought. That is to say, they are not considering the fundamental cause, just the effect.

Our technology may give us an illusion of superiority. If our present activities continue and the climate changes, it could easily happen that the entire grain belt of the Northern Hemisphere could become a desert, and in that case America would become very poor. The whole world would starve. Billions of people might die.

ME: One of the problems is that we don't really feel we are in the same boat. We pay lip service to the idea sometimes – we imagine that there are no countries and that the world is one – but this does not go very deep into the consciousness from which our actions ultimately arise.

DB: The isolation comes from the way we think. We are drawing false boundaries between ourselves and other people, and we experience these boundaries in our feelings. Unless our thinking changes, any change of feeling can't really be sustained, and so, as you have said, the overall change will not be very significant.

Even if we were to take some concrete practical steps to reforest Africa and to do all sorts of other things – stop the emissions that produce acid rain, reduce the production of carbon dioxide, and so on – still, vast numbers of poor people are going to be driven to do all sorts of things against the ecological balance unless we all feel responsible for them. And the basic pattern of our thought is that we do not feel this way. The ordinary, everyday person has an everyday family life and an everyday working life and does not think that way. Most of what you can generally think and read has it the other way. We have to notice this, and we have to bring things up and ask, for example, "Do you really not care that your grandchildren and those who follow them are going to starve to death and fight for the little that may be left, as long as you can have your hamburgers today?" Most people will agree, of course, that this can't be right. But the disk keeps pushing away that question, saying or implying that it's not an important question. The disk generally determines what questions seem to be the most important.

This is in part because most people lack the ability to grasp abstractions; that is one of the problems. Abstractions are actually very significant. In fact, abstractions have produced science and technology with all these problems. The fact that health has improved and the birth rate has gone up, the nuclear problems, the carbon dioxide – it's all due to abstractions. But people don't take them very seriously. Our education has not developed in us the ability to grasp the importance of abstractions. It is, on the whole, a very poor education anyway, and this is indeed part of the overall problem. I think we'll have to begin with those who can grasp abstractions, and we'll then have to try to bring these abstractions to wide public notice in a way that people can understand. And that requires creative action. That becomes part of the task, which is not only to understand these abstractions but to understand how to make them alive in the present to people generally.

ME: Can you explain this more fully?

DB: To *abstract* means literally to take something away, to separate something from its context. It's

very similar to the word *exact*. The question is, Why should you want to take something away from its context? This is what thought is always doing. It picks on something that seems to be relevant and important and tries to discuss this in the abstract, because that simplifies it and enables us to focus on the main point. The opposite of the abstract is the concrete. The word concrete comes from the Latin word *conscrescent*, meaning "grown together". You may imagine a jungle with a vast amount of concrete reality. You are generally, however, interested not in the whole jungle, but rather in certain animals or certain plants. In your mind you abstract a plant out of that vast jungle and say, "My mind is on that plant, I want to find that plant, because I want to eat it." You can see here the importance of abstraction. Even animals must abstract what is relevant in this jungle.

Reality is everything concrete and is much too much to be grasped by the mind in detail, so you make abstractions – call that foreground – and leave the rest as background, which you don't notice very much. In this process of abstraction, the word calls attention to something and gives it shape. For example, we have a very patterned carpet here in this room. Once I lost a coin on this carpet and couldn't see it. But I saw a glint, and as soon as I saw this I saw the coin. The glint enabled me to abstract the coin from the carpet; otherwise, it was lost in the details of the pattern.

We are constantly even in such elementary ways using abstraction, and we build on that. Indeed, every name is an abstraction of a class or category like water, air, fire. Even the name of a person is an abstraction – it doesn't tell you all about the person; you usually associate with it a few things about that person.

Knowledge is built up from such abstractions, which are then abstracted yet further. For example, you have chairs, tables, bookcases, and you abstract that as furniture. You can abstract the furniture further as material objects, and you can go on in this way to more and more general abstractions. This hierarchy of abstractions enables you to reason.

By abstracting you do two things: first of all, you leave out the vast complexity that you can't handle, and secondly, you begin to put some order into it, a logical coherent order, which enables you to reason. The word *reason* is based on the Latin *ratio*. This can be a numerical ratio, as with two numbers, like three over four. But a ratio can also be taken qualitatively: as A is related to B, so C is related to D. For example, as two things are related in thought, they are related in reality. Using abstract ratio, or reason, you can start from some fact and come to a conclusion.

Without abstraction we couldn't function; thought would be of no use; there would be no point in it. The choice of abstractions may be partly by memory, which tells you what is important, but it should also involve direct perception, to see whether the object of our thought really is as we think, or whether our thought is not working coherently. But if you are too stuck to your thought and identified with it, you can't change it by such perception.

So we really need to be able to change our abstractions when it is necessary to do so. But to do this, we have to see that they are abstractions. This is often difficult, because abstractions, though insubstantial in themselves, can produce substantial concrete results that, in a cursory inspection, give the appearance of an independently existent reality. For example, we may feel that a country is such a reality. But without

the abstract thought of a nation, the country would vanish. If people didn't know that they belonged to a certain nation, there would be no country, in spite of all the houses, factories, legislation, and so on. Nobody would know that it was all related, that it made up a particular country that, for example, must be defended at all costs.

The essential point is, then, that abstractions can produce sustained concrete results, and that thought loses track of this. In a way that we have described earlier, it then calls such concrete results independent realities. It then says, "I'm only telling you about this concrete reality." This leads to confusion. It means, for example, that you might now try to correct this supposedly independent reality while your abstractions are working constantly to *prevent* you from correcting it. Indeed, they are constantly making you recreate it as it was before, while at the same time you make another abstraction that says you should change it. That may happen in a revolution. We see the terrible mess in society. We take this mess as a concrete reality independent of thought, and we make an abstraction of a revolution to change it. However, we have all sorts of other abstractions in human relationships, such as who's the boss, who has power, and so on. So the revolution produces basically the same sort of society, with just a change in its details.

ME: You are calling for a new kind of intelligence.

DB: Yes. We need a new kind of intelligence because we have created a world that requires it. In the Stone Age the ordinary practical intelligence was good enough. People then had an instinctive sort of intelligence developed somewhat by culture. But today we have created a complex world based on the abstractions of thought. To deal with nature we need a certain kind of intelligence, but to deal with thought we need a much higher sort of intelligence.

We tend to think that thought *is* this sort of intelligence, but it isn't. The key point about thought is that it is like the program, the disk, that responds to the situation. There is no reason why a disk should respond intelligently – a thing might change, and the disk might no longer be appropriate. It responds quickly and automatically according to what has been programmed into it. Similarly, what we have been thinking and learning is programmed into our memory. It's not merely a picture of what happened in the past but a program for potential action. That program is extremely subtle; to deal with it takes much more subtlety than to deal with the objects the program deals with.

Here we come to what I call the *process* of thought. Thought has a content, that is, a certain substance or meaning. In the past, people may have just prayed to the rain god. Now we say that the weather is a process. We don't understand it fully, but at least we see that it is a process. And insofar as we do understand it, we can predict it to some extent, and adapt to it. We are even beginning to look into the process of maintaining or changing climate, and we can now act more intelligently in this regard if we want to.

So we understand that there is this process of the weather. But as for thought, nobody ever looks at it. We just take it for granted, the way people used to do with the weather. It's as if we supposed that inside us there is a thought god who produces thought, according to arbitrary whim. That thought god could be called "I" or "me" or "the self". Thus it is implied that each of us is somehow in control of his or her own thoughts. But what I am suggesting is that, as a process, thought moves,

for the most part, on its own, and that there is little possibility of this process coming to order until we understand it fairly well.

Development, which is called progress, has become a menace. As long as there is money to be made by developing and money available to do it, it seems almost impossible to stop it. You may resist it for a while, but they are going to keep working until they find a way around it. That is, again, the way we think. Development is thought to be absolutely necessary, so that we mustn't stop it, no matter what it does to destroy the ecological balance of nature or its beauty, or to turn our cities into unlivable jungles of concrete. But we've got to stop this heedless rush into development, because that way lies a meaningless life and eventually disaster.

There is hardly a politician who would dare say that sooner or later this sort of growth must stop. Yet you can see that such growth must ultimately destroy the world. As we pointed our earlier, if all the nations in the world tried to obtain the present Western standard of living, our planet would be devastated. Just to consider one point alone, the amount of carbon dioxide would multiply by many times. Indeed, you can apply the sort of calculation that I have made about population growth to the economy instead. If the economy grows by 2.5% per year, which is very small, in a thousand years it will have grown ten thousand million times! We will have to stop it somewhere, and it is clear that we have passed the point at which we should begin seriously to consider what would be a right approach to this whole question. For it makes no sense to go on giving growth such a high priority, so that it ultimately overrides almost everything else. What is of primary importance is to have a healthy ecological balance in nature and a good quality of life for everyone. Within the context of these requirements we can then see the kind and degree of growth that is called for.

It is very hard for people to change their thought about all this, however. What prevents us from stopping our present unintelligent sort of growth is ultimately the thought that the continuation of such growth is absolutely necessary and that we can't live without it. But we can live without it, as long as we don't make these material products the main point of life. For example, we have to reorganize life fundamentally so that we don't flood our roads with cars. We have to have other ways of getting around, or perhaps we may not even get around so much. We may instead try to make our living places, our cities, so good that we don't have to rush off to somewhere else. All that would mean reorganizing life almost totally. The general momentum of the last few hundred years is in the wrong direction. People have thought mainly of progress, growth and development as the prime goals of our society. But this movement has by now become destructive. One could indeed say that Western countries have already carried their current lines of development too far, while the other countries cannot stand much further development of this kind.

It is clear that we have a crisis developing. And if we go on with this momentum, the end is certain; it is only a question of when. Will it be in fifty years? Or in a hundred years? It's hard to estimate. But you can see that if we continue to grow for a thousand years, we'll have overgrown ten thousand million times – there will be nothing left on this planet or on any planet around it. You see the power of that sort of growth? It has tremendous power – it is only an abstraction, but it has all that power.

But how is this abstraction to change? People don't see the meaning of abstract thought. They're not used to thinking about abstract thought. As I've said earlier, we have got to develop the ability to see what abstraction is, to see its power. These abstractions are doing the job. These abstractions are actually concrete realities when considered as an actual process. That is to say, the process of thought itself is a concrete reality whose product is abstractions. This concrete process is running away with us. The first thing is to become conscious and aware that this is happening, to find ways to enable people to appreciate the importance of these abstractions. They are not really just shadowy abstractions; they are being projected by a concrete process that produces very big concrete results.

HARD RAIN PROJECT

The Hard Rain Project is run from my home in London, from where a small team arranges exhibitions and illustrated talks and keeps this book updated. The exhibition is the key element because it's seen by accidental visitors. People come across the banner by chance in a botanic garden or city centre and are drawn into the debate about our future. So far 12 million have seen Hard Rain on every continent and future exhibitions will include a new banner presenting solutions to the issues it illustrates. We will have succeeded if people new to these issues make their voices heard; and if those who are already concerned make their voices heard a little louder. The world has arrived at a narrow window of opportunity to avert disasters that are increasingly imminent and ever closer to home.

It's not always easy putting pressure on our leaders. By way of gentle persuasion I sent copies of the Hard Rain book to every prime minister in the world – and to President George W. Bush, care of the US embassy in London. It came back three days later; the envelope marked "Not known at this address". Replies from leaders who did respond can be seen on our website.

Hard Rain started by accident but now it's a full-time job financed hand-to-mouth by illustrated talks for NGOs, businesses, and public meetings. I will continue to mail out the book to decision-makers and invite them to commit to effective action. Those in power are realists, reacting to the realities of the political systems we have built, and they need a constituency to pass legislation that will help create a sustainable world.

Please join me and encourage your government to take decisive action to meet targets to reduce CO_2 emissions, to finally deliver the target of 0.7% of GDP as official aid set out by the UN fifty years ago, and to negotiate equitable trade agreements with poor countries so they can develop businesses that will lift people out of poverty. Support business leaders who are moving towards ways of using resources in a sustainable way. Boycott those who do not.

Hard Rain shows there are not many problems, but one problem with many solutions. The one problem: aligning human systems with natural systems.

We are not going to pretend that there are solutions to all our problems – many scientists and environmental experts acknowledge privately, if not publicly, that there is a price to pay for the damage we have done to the earth's life-support systems. There is a good deal of discussion and disagreement about that price, but all are agreed that every step we take towards sustainable living will lessen the impact of a natural backlash that will diminish everyone's quality of life.

We need leaders who are visionaries who can see the real threats behind complex syndromes and can explain these to people, build coalitions and lay out solutions. Most politicians and business leaders have failed to seriously engage with sustainable issues. That is why we all have to act. But it's not just political action that's needed. We are dependent on nature, but most of us have lost touch with the natural world. We need to reconnect with the planet. Awareness of the intricate web of life that makes civilizations viable is the first step on the path to a sustainable culture we can all participate in.

In December 2008, UK Energy and Climate Change Minister Ed Miliband told the *Guardian* that a "popular mobilization" was needed to help politicians push through an agreement to limit carbon emissions:

"There will be some people saying 'we can't go ahead with an agreement on climate change, it's not the biggest priority'. And, therefore, what you need is countervailing forces. Some of those countervailing forces come from popular mobilization. I think back to Make Poverty History... and that was a mass movement that was necessary to get the agreement. In terms of climate change, it's even more difficult. There are people who have legitimate concerns, whether it's businesses in Europe who are concerned about competitiveness, or people who [ask] 'is it really necessary to do this now?'

"When you think about all the big historic movements, from the suffragettes, to anti-apartheid, to sexual equality in the 1960s, all the big political movements had popular mobilization. Maybe it's an odd thing for someone in government to say, but I just think there's a real opportunity and a need here. Political change comes from leadership and popular mobilization. And you need both of them."

Go for a walk, look at the trees and the sky, consider how those of us in the rich world – and the newly rich in developing nations – can learn to live better with less. Then go home and start writing letters.

On his election as president in 1932 Franklin D. Roosevelt told a group of reformers, "I agree with you, I want to do it, now make me do it."

EXHIBITION

Presented as a 60-metre banner, the Hard Rain exhibition has been shown at over 50 venues around the world including botanic gardens, museums and city parks in East and West Europe, Scandinavia, South Africa, Australia and America.

So why is Hard Rain so stunning and so moving, and why does it feel so right? Part of the answer, of course, lies in the quality of the visual images, mostly by Edwards himself, but also by Sebastião Salgado, Chris Steele-Perkins and other photographers.

But the thematic bundling of these images with Dylan's song could still seem gauche or exploitative were it not for two factors. The most important of these is the sheer brilliance of the dialogue Edwards has created between the words and the images, the way they synthesise into some third form that combines the stillness of a picture with the urgency of a ballad. Edwards' conjunctions are so carefully and thoughtfully constructed that they enforce on the viewer a kind of tact that wards off mere voyeurism.
Fintan O'Toole, *Irish Times*

Royal Botanic Garden, Edinburgh

Edon Project, Cornwall

United Nations Building, New York

Kirstenbosch National Botanical Garden, Cape Town

Chester Zoo, Upton, Cheshire

Canberra International Arboretum and Gardens

University of St Thomas, St Paul, Minnesota

Syracuse University, New York

National Botanic Gardens, Dublin

DOCUMENTARY PRESENTATION

The Hard Rain documentary presentation is a personal account of the environmental journey I began in 1969. The presentation opens with Bob Dylan's "A Hard Rain's A-Gonna Fall". The exhibition pictures are projected to the song that goes on to explore the state of the world and its people, and brings alive the policies, technologies and lifestyle changes we need to reinvent the modern world so that it is compatible with nature.

Hard Rain lasts 50 minutes and is illustrated with over 200 striking images from around the world.

To book the exhibition or the presentation, please contact the Hard Rain office.

Hard Rain Project
199 Shooters Hill Road
London SE3 8UL
United Kingdom

mark@hardrainproject.com
+44 (0)20 8858 8307
www.hardrainproject.com

Hard Rain is one of the most powerful presentations I have ever seen – and it has a huge impact on people.
Jonathon Porritt, *Founding Director, Forum for the Future*

What is refreshing is that Mark doesn't paint the situation as hopeless. He highlights real changes governments, industry and individuals can make that are potentially highly effective.
Alex Ritson, *Senior Editorial Advisor, BBC Global News*

Thank you for your impressive Hard Rain presentation for the IPCC scientists in Berlin. Although the pictures are hard-hitting and disturbing they gave me something that had been missing from the conference. I was astonished at how deeply I was touched and involved by the careful and intelligent combination of words, music and pictures.
Sonja Waldhausen, *research scientist, Berlin*

FEEDBACK

Hard Rain is both a tremendous achievement and an incredibly troubling book to read – an unrelenting catalogue of burnt and barren landscapes, shrunken ice caps and devastated, dislocated lives.

Page by page it conjures up the terrible consequences of unchecked climate change – a human catastrophe that is quite unprecedented in our history, and one that we can no longer afford to deny.

Already, climate change and the competition for natural resources are destroying livelihoods, creating refugees and stoking conflicts right around the world. To allow this disaster to deepen further would be an unforgivable injustice – for whilst it is the richest countries that have caused this degradation, it is the poorest who are suffering its worst effects.

So if Hard Rain is a photographic elegy it is also an impassioned cry for change. Forceful, dramatic and disturbing, it is driven by what Martin Luther King called "the fierce urgency of now" – and I believe the call for a truly global response to climate change is an idea whose time has finally come.

Rt Hon Gordon Brown MP, *Prime Minister of the United Kingdom*

This is a book of powerful words and some even more powerful images. It reflects the thoughts of a generation who do not just want prosperity for themselves but who want progress for the poor as well, and who know we need a sustainable environment, not just to pass on to the next generation but to make life better in this generation too. Tackling climate change is not a distant and remote concern, but an urgent priority.

The truth is that, when it comes to these challenges, we are all in it together – we all have a role to play. The decisions we make, for example, about shopping, travelling and living all make a difference.

So the lesson from this book is not only of the damage we are causing, but of the shared responsibility we all have to respond – and to do those things which, step by step, can make a real difference.

Rt Hon David Cameron MP, *Leader of the Conservative Party*

This is a moving and thought-provoking book, which illustrates, through the use of powerful images, the undeniable ongoing relevance of Dylan's lyrics. Environmental and human poverty is today at a level that Dylan could not have envisaged when he wrote those disturbing lyrics some forty years ago. Yet many of the world leaders, those who have the ability to affect a change, have failed to take care of the needs of the many. This must end now.

Scientists agree that we now have less than ten years to make the changes that will prevent the earth's temperature entering its danger zone – the point of no return. Politicians and individuals must stop passing the buck and be part of the solution rather than the problem. A zero carbon future is a happy, healthy, equitable future, so what are we waiting for?

Another world is possible, and hopefully Hard Rain will bring this message to a new audience that will start taking action.

Dr Caroline Lucas MEP, *Leader of the Green Party of England and Wales*

Each day I avert my eyes and steer my thoughts away from the inevitable outcome. I ignore the headlong rush which sweeps us all along and bury my head in silence and in shame. The monumental extent of that which brings about our end has seemed unassailable. Increasingly I have been unable to engage. Everywhere I look I see my own participation in this race to, and over, the precipice.

This book inspires me to try and stand

again. To know that others share this bleakest outlook brings a ray of hope.

At first I thought that Dylan's lines should not be illustrated. I was wrong. Sincerely,
Christy Moore

A wonderful and powerful broadside. It reminds me of Munch's *Scream*. And of what Bertrand Russell called mankind's "silly cleverness".

And yet it's only part of the picture. Yes, perhaps the biggest part – we are indeed a greedy, stupid, selfish species. But we are also generous and imaginative and inspiring and self-sacrificing. And this side of humanity barely gets a mention. Vietnam dragged on for year after miserable year; tens of millions protested the war in Iraq before it even started. This didn't stop the invasion, but things are changing, perhaps faster and more fundamentally than any of us realize. There are millions of seeds of hope: tens of millions.

But maybe that is for another of the books you promise. I hope so.
Jon Tinker, *Executive Director, Panos Institute of Canada*

Here is our world as for most of humanity it has become, and as the world's leaders would rather not acknowledge. It is brought to us through a poem that cuts as poetry must through the facts to the meaning of things, and by photographs that capture the passing scene in one sharp permanent image – and also the emotion of it, and the reasons that lie behind it. We doubtless need statistics and learned analyses if we are to get to grips with the world but most of all we need to give a damn, and here we can see, if we take just a few minutes, why we should. This is the power of art.
Colin Tudge

"A Hard Rain's A-Gonna Fall" was one of the defining protest songs of the sixties. While its original inspiration was the threat of nuclear meltdown, it has been effortlessly composed into a modern context by Mark Edwards, whose plangent photographic essay is as moving a piece of work as I have seen for a long time. It is also important and timely because it is the 60s generation who now make up the bulk of the establishment. A reminder of how, little by little, our capacity for righteous anger has been eroded by the years of compromise so many of us have lived through, may just move us once more to remember what it is like to yell at the top of our voices, "enough". This disturbing, powerfully moving work is a masterpiece that summons up the ghosts of our past and a vision of the future that is ours to change. Regret and optimism make strange bedfellows, but great artists have always known this.
Tim Smit, *Chief Executive and co-founder, The Eden Project*

Someone once wrote that politics without dissent has a corpse in its mouth, and that all of us inclined to either the Right or the Left need to recognize the importance of a much wider version of subversion. We all live in a world where we are told forcibly that the alternatives to the present way of doing things are not feasible, that to believe otherwise is suspect, and the "wise" (politicians, economists) know best. So the actors of freedom, the dissenters and protestors always seem oppressed by the talkers of freedom.

I have found dissent and protest is a lonely business, and yet that seems to fuel an enthusiasm for rhetoric. In anger, anguish, fear and pride it is the words, the language, the symbols, and the music that can often move you to action.
Dame Anita Roddick, *founder of The Body Shop*

I read Hard Rain and thought it was compelling. I read it again and it was more compelling. Three months later I read it a third time while sitting in a taxi caught in a traffic jam and it was like a kick in the guts, a terrible vision of the apocalyptic future that climate change could wreak on humanity. The suffering of millions of refugees fleeing flooded or drought-stricken lands, the breakdown of economies, then civilization. And then the rule of the jungle. All these could be consequences of climate change. Mark Edwards' photos and Dylan's lyrics combine as if made for each other to convey a hideous future.

But it doesn't have to be like this, the future is not fixed.
Harry Bruhns, UK

Saving the environment will hardly be achieved by forcing nation states to act or persuading scientists that, after a technology of destruction, it is time to develop a technology of salvation. Nation states may be part of the problem, in that in their myopic attention to limited territories they may believe that competition with other states will make the winners survive and the losers succumb. In an extreme, if realistic, version of such competition the poisons produced in developed countries can be transferred to developing ones, a form of environmental imperialism. There are only losers in this competition and, as David Bohm wonderfully argues, nationalism is for the environment a contemporary form of plague.

Scientists, in their turn, may compound the problem, as their professional performance is measured through the contribution they make to economic growth. David Bohm's views echo what some theorists in Europe call "de-growth", an economic initiative which incorporates a radical critique of the very notions of development, output, national product or, for that matter, added value and profit. If these notions have acquired "objective" existence and universal validity in economic discourse, this is not due to their being part of the inescapable reality, but to the way in which "thought" has managed to isolate them and turn them into abstractions. Here, Bohm's ideas are crucial for the development of a global environmental consciousness. Our thought does not reflect reality, it contributes to its creation. If we focus on other aspects and variables, these may acquire universal validity as well: our gaze may be turned away from growth and economic performance, and onto solidarity and life. Hard Rain is a superb contribution to the debate on the environment. The compelling images provided by Mark Edwards, the moving verses of Bob Dylan, and the thought-provoking observations of David Bohm give us a beautiful message of civic hope.
Lucia and **Vincenzo Ruggiero**, London

It has been pointed out that photographs describe everything, but explain nothing. How true. Hard Rain achieves an extraordinary feat of bringing together a diverse and remarkable selection of photographs, and by placing them into the context of this book, making them explain a very great deal. Not necessarily what they were originally intended to explain, as with Dylan's lyrics, but something that all their authors can be proud to participate in, and feel solidarity with this message.

Bring this book to the attention of your friends, and spread it around.
Chris Steele-Perkins, London

I came across the exhibition on a sunny day while out with my children in Edinburgh and was profoundly moved and dismayed by the images and text. The power of this exhibition in the setting of Princes Street Gardens was intense and made me feel both insignificant and empowered. I did not share these images with my children who were happily playing but it is they and future generations that should compel all of us to act, however insignificant we may feel.
Shian Randall, Scotland

It's a grim picture, but Hard Rain also inspires hope. It gives readers a sense of purpose and an almost palpable desire to do something positive, something that will make a difference.
Calvin Jones, *Cork Evening Echo*

In seconds I was hooked, desperate to save the planet... Hard Rain is a harrowing onslaught on our shared responsibility for climate change, for poverty (both spiritual and material), for habitat loss and for the abuse of basic human rights. The message is that environmental and human poverty reinforce each other. Many sensitive people are aware, to at least some extent, that if only through their consumption patterns they contribute to the raping of our environment and to appalling mistreatment of our fellow beings, human and non-human. These images, from many countries and many contexts, must heighten

that awareness, and bring it into acute focus. They illustrate a world gone desperately wrong.
Harry Reid, *The Herald* (Glasgow)

I am an 18-year-old senior at Mira Costa High School in Manhattan Beach, California. My father got this book when he was in Paris, where Mark Edwards spoke. The first moments I opened the book I could feel the impact it made upon me. As I flipped through the pages my eyes started to fill with tears. As I read the last lines, all I could think of was the hard rain coming down from my eyes. I shared this book with my Government and Psychology teacher, and we read it out loud to the class. The intense look in everyone's eyes was amazing. Five kids I didn't even know came up to me later that day and said thank you for showing that because it made such an impact on them. Thank you so much.
Nikki Price, Manhattan Beach, California

I just listened to the original song whilst reading your book. I cried.

I am an Environmental Sciences student, aware of many of the facts and the situation we find ourselves in through study, but this didn't diminish the power of your message. I just hope projects such as this can change attitudes quickly enough to have an effect.

Politicians talk of targets and why they should be in power – environmentalism used to gain votes, but the result would be the same. No change. Why do the people in power not understand that their money and businesses are worth nothing if the planet dies?
Mathieu Pendergast, UK

The images drew a huge emotion from myself and others around me. Seeing something so raw and descriptive has really hit your message home. I left with a copy of the book and a constant reminder of what is often overlooked in society today, vowing to become much more aware of what difference each of us can make. Additionally, a few weeks ago my girlfriend told me about a class trip from her school to the Eden Project. The teachers were all back at the bus and getting increasingly anxious that the children had not returned yet as time was running out. When they eventually turned up it turned out that they had not been able to draw themselves away from the Hard Rain display – so your message is getting out to the people that will make the change.
Paul Hassall, Ipswich

What will it take to derail business as usual and engage the moment? The facts are in, now is the time for those who are sensitive to the truth and the growing awareness of the peril we are about to confront, to speak out and lead the way into a brave new world.
James Leighton, Portland, Oregon

Jesus… When you have seen Hard Rain, life stops for a moment. I don't know how people can go on like this. I listened to the song as well. It was so moving. Even at the age of twelve, I find it hard to comprehend this. I cried over it.
Meera Patel, UK

In London, the common will of the people can convince the city governors to reserve parks from development. It is not so hard for those in power to withstand pressure to cash in on the value of Hyde Park. But such valuable political action is simply invisible when faced with the value of the atmosphere.

The message of this book, and of the project itself, is spot on. We all need to push for global governance that values a global environment.
Roger Yates, London

I picked up a copy of Hard Rain when I visited the Eden Project. The combination of words and pictures spoke to me instantly, at a deep level. I was inspired and motivated to see in this work the accomplishment of evoking powerful emotion by giving words a context and pictures a voice. The message of being "the change you want to see in the world" resonated with me. Hard Rain is a beautiful, tender, honest and painful piece of work.
Amanda Milligan, Manchester

We see the disasters that have happened, we know the catastrophes that approach. We have the chance now to invent a new future for humanity. But what does that future look like? What do we want our common future to be?

Steve Gale, Australia

Do we have a planetary mentality?

The last Chief, Plenty Coups, of the tribe of Crow Indians died in 1920. The Crows were warriors first and foremost and were known for staking out their ever-changing grounds for buffalo with "coup sticks" – the word coup being used in the sense of "pulling off a coup". Once a warrior planted a coup stick, it marked a boundary that if transgressed by an outsider would give rise to a fight, if necessary to the death. For the men of the Crow tribe to stake out hunting grounds in this way and to successfully defend them against all comers was the highest honour and virtue – in fact it seemed to be the only one they aspired to.

What happened to the Crow after the buffalo went, slaughtered en masse by the white men? Well, Chief Plenty Coups put it this way: "After this, nothing happened." The tribe, as a culture, simply disintegrated.

How different was the Crow culture, in its prime, from the culture of the modern nation? To take one example, the Falklands war showed the British determined to defend their disputed lands, and passionately so in the case of their Prime Minister, Mrs Thatcher. And the modern nation often extends its territorial frontiers to embrace what is called its "spheres of interest" – oil-producing countries being a clear example. Dying in defence of one's country or its "interests" is regarded as heroic and earns the hero the highest national honours. All this is regarded by most of us as normal. So how different are we from the Crow tribe? And will our national cultures survive the new planetary challenge they now face?

Relevant to that was a recent programme on US television describing the effect on the earth of "global dimming". This refers to the reduction in sunlight reaching the earth's surface due to clouds of pollutant particles caused mainly by the industries of the US and Europe. According to this documentary these clouds effectively displaced in the 60s and 70s the monsoon in the Sahel (Africa south of the Sahara) and led to mass starvation of its inhabitants. Pollution in the US and Europe of the kind that produced this disaster has since been reduced and the Sahel monsoon has returned.

But this blatant example of the catastrophic effects of human pollution on people who had no hand in causing it shows that, without a planetary policy on climate change and pollution, the prospects for new kinds of human strife and terrorism are immense. Also, the fact that pandemics, such as the possible one of Asian bird flu, are more likely to emerge in very poor countries and then spread rapidly to rich ones through air travel means that a planetary medical policy is likely to be the only way to prevent this. Well, we have the World Health Organization: but will it be able to do everything needed?

Both of these examples, and there are many others, strongly suggest that the tribal-national model, brought about by our genes as an appropriate means of survival in the environment of past millennia, is hopelessly inadequate as an adaptation to the present planetary challenges. However, we are nonetheless able, as the evolutionary biologist Richard Dawkins puts it, "to rebel against our genes", and he has called this "an unexpected bonus" at our present point in history. And what this present point in history demands, according to a recent UK government report on climate change, is "unprecedented international cooperation", nothing less than a new human mentality – one that transcends our so far-rooted and neurotically obsessive allegiances to national interests and identity.

The problem is this. It is quite clearly now impossible to defend our national interests without simultaneously taking into account the interests of other nations and of the planet as a whole. This is an inescapable fact and a wholly new way of looking at the world and our position in it. Put another way, unless xenophobia gives way to species loyalty – a deeply felt sense of all of us being in the same boat – we are very unlikely to achieve "unprecedented international cooperation" and are more likely to have unprecedented conflict due to outmoded economic, political, and religious divisions.

Old ways of thinking don't work anymore. And it will need a real mental leap to change them. Are we capable of making that leap?
David Skitt

There is a tide in the affairs of men
Which, taken at the flood, leads on to fortune;
Omitted, all the voyage of their life
Is bound in shallows and in miseries.
On such a full sea are we now afloat,
And we must take the current when it serves,
Or lose our ventures.
William Shakespeare

Hard Rain shows me that we're already bumping the bottom of our boat in the shallows.

Remarkably, if man were removed from this planet, paradise would be the result – so much for technology improving our living conditions. We need more Dylan and Mark Edwards protest campaigns to get governments to change.
Kevin Watson, Scotland

Australia is a striking example of what happens to the earth as it ages and if it is not actively cared for. Australia is almost uninhabitable in the interior because it's old and has not been renewed. The rest of the world will eventually follow if resources and land are not actually husbanded.
Sheila Armstrong, Santa Fe and Perth

I bought your book from the Eden Project. Some of the images are disturbing. I have three small children and I fear that when they grow up the world will be ruined. When I grew up in Bolton every winter was very cold with snow and ice. Even though I live in Cornwall now, the winters are very mild. My children have never seen proper snow. Five thousand people were killed in the Indonesia earthquake. A few lines mentioned on the news, nothing more – disgusting. I seem to recall the 9/11 attacks taking over the airwaves for days. I applaud your efforts but I'm afraid this generation will be known as the selfish ones, maybe it is time nature took back the earth, man is obviously incapable of looking after it.
Andrew Oakes, Truro

Hard Rain shows in painful detail the destruction of planet and life that climate change has already brought about and what the future holds if we carry on regardless. If any book can shake people out of their complacency, this is the one. Make your libraries buy it, show it to your friends, family and co-workers, show it to everyone you meet every day. Read it and weep. And then do something about it.
Muriel Lumb, Book STEPs, Bantry, Co. Cork, Republic of Ireland

I bought your book after visiting the Eden Project and seeing your exhibition; a procession of visitors, quiet and visibly moved by the photographs and words. If we each could spend just one minute of one day doing something to make a difference, then collectively, what a difference we could make.
Arlene Harris, Rossendale, Lancashire

I walked along the line of posters, words piled on words, image on image. I knew the lyrics; Dylan was part of the soundtrack of my life, yet somehow the apocalyptic vision was just that, a warning rather than a description. Suddenly this was a reality. Now each line of the song was real and by the time I reached the end there were silent tears running down my face.

We must act – as individuals and collectively. Regret what we have done and what we have failed to do. Take action and get angry at those who don't. Can I tell my grandchildren that I knew but did nothing?
Geoff Brace, Ipswich

An outstanding example of passionate commitment to remake our world, Hard Rain is a call to action that has already moved millions of people throughout the world, pushing them to confront a harsh reality, but also awakening their desire to react to the devastation of the planet.
Eric Falt, *Director, Outreach Division, UN Department of Public Information*

The hard reality is that the hard rain of environmental destruction continues to fall and global efforts are not anywhere near what is required, dramatically required, at this point. And political will is still very much in short supply.
Olav Kjorven, *Director for Development Policy, UNDP*

See a wider selection of readers' comments, and add your own at **www.hardrainproject.com**

RESOURCES

Books (alphabetical, by author)

Non-fiction/general

Last Chance to See by Douglas Adams and Mark Cawardine (William Heinemann, 1990; reissue Arrow Books, 2009)

Adapting to Climate Change: Thresholds, Values, Governance edited by Neil Adger, Irene Lorenzoni and Karen O'Brien (Cambridge University Press, 2009).

The Great Illusion: A Study of the Relation of Military Power in Nations to Their Economic and Social Advantage by Sir Norman Angell (William Heinemann, 1911; Cosimo Classics, 2007).

Understanding the Present: An Alternative History of Science by Brian Appleyard (Picador, 1992).

The Peregrine by J.A. Baker (Harper Collins 1967; NYRB Classics, 2005).

The Coming Global Superstorm by Art Bell and Whitley Strieber (Atria, 1999).

Changing Consciousness by David Bohm and Mark Edwards (Harper Collins, 1989).

Earth Under Fire: How Global Warming is Changing the World by Gary Braasch (University of California Press, 2007).

Beyond Malthus: The Nineteen Dimensions of the Population Challenge by Lester R. Brown, Gary Gardner and Brian Halweil (Earthwatch, 1999).

Eco-Economy: Building an Economy for the Earth by Lester R. Brown (Norton, 2001).

Plan B 3.0: Mobilizing to Save Civilization by Lester Brown (revised edition, WW Norton & Co, 2008).

Global Warning: The Last Chance for Change by Paul Brown (Guardian Books/A&C Black, 2006).

The Storm: The World Economic Crisis and What it Means by Vince Cable (Atlantic Books, 2009).

Silent Spring by Rachel Carson (Houghton Mifflin, 1962; Penguin Modern Classics, 2000).

The Politics of the Environment: Ideas, Activism, Policy by Neil Carter (Cambridge University Press, 2007).

The End of the Line: How Overfishing is Changing the World and What We Eat by Charles Clover (Ebury Press, 2004; University of California Press, 2008).

Fatal Misconception: The Struggle to Control World Population by Michael Connelly (Harvard University Press, 2008).

The Science and Politics of Global Climate Change: A Guide to the Debate by Andrew E. Dessler and Edward A. Parson (Cambridge University Press, 2006).

Collapse: How Societies Choose to Fail or Survive by Jared Diamond (Allen Lane, 2005).

The Atlas of Climate Change: Mapping the World's Greatest Challenge by Kirstin Dow and Thomas E. Downing (Earthscan, 2006).

Chronicles: Volume One by Bob Dylan (Simon & Schuster, 2004).

Edge Futures by The Edge Group: a series of five books exploring the impact of climate change on different aspects of our lives. *Work and the City* by Frank Duffy, *Transport and Neighbourhoods* by Hank Dittmar, *Education and Creativity* by Simon Foxell and William J. Mitchell, *Living and Community* by Geoff Mulgan, and *Globalism and Regionalism* by Jonathon Porritt (Black Dog Publishing, 2008).

One with Nineveh: Politics, Consumption and the Human Future by Paul R. and Anne H. Ehrlich, (Island Press, 2004).

The Weather Makers: The History and Future Impact of Climate Change by Tim Flannery (Allen Lane, 2006).

Hot, Flat and Crowded: Why the World Needs a Green Revolution – and How We Can Renew Our Global Future by Thomas L. Friedman (Allen Lane, 2008).

The Ethics of Climate Change: Right and Wrong in a Warming World by James Garvey (Continuum, 2008).

The Politics of Climate Change by Anthony Giddens (Polity Press, 2009).

Earthrise: How We Can Heal Our Injured Planet by Herbert Girardet (Paladin, 1992).

A Renewable World: Energy, Ecology, Equality (A Report for the World Future Council) by Herbert Girardet and Miguel Mendonça (Green Books, 2009).

The Sixth Extinction: Journeys Among the Lost and Left Behind by Terry Glavin (Thomas Dunne Books/Saqi, 2007).

How to Live a Low Carbon Life: The Individual's Guide to Stopping Climate Change by Chris Goodall, (Earthscan, 2007).

Ten Technologies to Save the Planet by Chris Goodall (Green Profile, 2008).

The Green Guide for Business by Chris Goodall (Green Profile, 2009).

Refashioning Nature: Food, Ecology and Culture by David Goodman and Michael Redclift (Routledge, 1991).

Earth in the Balance by Al Gore (Houghton Mifflin, 1992).

An Inconvenient Truth: The Planetary Emergency of Global Warming and What We Can Do About It by Al Gore (Rodale Books/Bloomsbury, 2006).

The Assault on Reason: How the Politics of Blind Faith Subvert Wise Decision-Making by Al Gore (Penguin Putnam/Bloomsbury, 2007).

The Third Revolution by Paul Harrison (I.B. Tauris in association with Penguin Books, 1992).

Natural Capitalism by Paul Hawken, Amory Lovins and L. Hunter Lovins (Little, Brown, 1999).

Blessed Unrest: How the Largest Movement in the World Came Into Being and Why No One Saw It Coming by Paul Hawken (Viking, 2007).

Powerdown: Options and Actions for a Post-Carbon Society by Richard Heinberg (revised edition Clairview Books, 2007).

Peak Everything: Waking Up to the Century of Decline In Earth's Resources by Richard Heinberg (Clairview Books, 2007).

The Rough Guide to Climate Change by Robert Henson (revised edition Rough Guides, 2008).

Bob Dylan: Behind the Shades Revisited by Clinton Heylin (revised edition, Wiliam Morrow, 2001).

How We Can Save the Planet by Mayer Hillman (Penguin Books, 2004).

The Upside of Down by Thomas Homer-Dixon, (Island Press, 2006).

The Transition Handbook: From Oil Dependency to Local Resilience by Rob Hopkins (Green Books, 2008).

Global Warming: The Complete Briefing by John Houghton, (fourth edition Cambridge University Press, 2009).

Why We Disagree About Climate Change: Understanding Controversy, Inaction and Opportunity by Mike Hulme (Cambridge University Press, 2009).

The Green Collar Economy: How One Solution Can Fix Our Two Biggest Problems by Van Jones (HarperOne, 2008).

How Many Lightbulbs Does It Take to Change a Planet?: 95 Ways to Save Planet Earth by Tony Juniper (Quercus, 2007).

Global Warming i\$ Good for Business by K.B. Keilbach (Driver Books, 2009).

The Shock Doctrine: The Rise of Disaster Capitalism by Naomi Klein (Allen Lane, 2007).

Field Notes from a Catastrophe: Climate Change – Is Time Running Out? by Elizabeth Kolbert (Bloomsbury, 2006).

The Ending of Time by J. Krishnamurti and David Bohm (Victor Gollancz, 1985).

Freedom from the Known by J. Krishnamurti, edited by Mary Lutyens (Victor Gollancz, 1969).

All the Marvelous Earth by J. Krishnamurti (Krishnamurti Publications of America, 2000).

Facing a World in Crisis by J. Krishnamurti (Shambhala Publications, 2005).

On Nature and the Environment by J. Krishnamurti, (Victor Gollancz, 1992).

Krishnamurti's complete writings can be browsed at www.jkrishnamurti.org

The Long Emergency: Surviving the Converging Catastrophes of the Twenty-First Century by James Howard Kunstler (Atlantic Books, 2005).

Fixing Climate: The Story of Climate Science – and How to Stop Global Warming by Robert Kunzig and Wallace S. Broecker (Green Profile, 2008).

The Chaos Point: The World at the Crossroads by Ervin Laszlo (Hampton Roads/Piatkus, 2006).

The Sixth Extinction: Patterns of Life and the Future of Humankind by Richard E. Leakey and Roger Lewin (Doubleday, 1995).

The Carbon War: Dispatches from the End of the Oil Century by Jeremy Leggett (Allen Lane, 1999).

Half Gone: Oil, Gas, Hot Air and the Global Energy Crisis by Jeremy Leggett (Portobello Books, 2005).

Global Environmental Challenges of the Twenty-First Century edited by David Lorey (Scholarly Resources, 2002).

Gaia: A New Look at Life on Earth by James Lovelock (Oxford University Press, 1979).

The Revenge of Gaia: Why the Earth Is Fighting Back – and How We Can Still Save Humanity by James Lovelock (Allen Lane, 2006).

The Vanishing Face of Gaia by James Lovelock (Allen Lane, 2009).

The End of World Population Growth in the 21st Century: New Challenges for Human Capital Formation and Sustainable Development edited By Wolfgang Lutz, Warren C. Sanderson and Sergei Scherbov (Earthscan, 2004).

Carbon Counter by Mark Lynas (Collins, 2006).

High Tide: News from a Warming World by Mark Lynas (Flamingo, 2004).

Fragile Earth: Views of a Changing World by Mark Lynas, Tim Flannery et al. (Collins, 2006).

Six Degrees: Our Future on a Hotter Planet by Mark Lynas (Fourth Estate, 2007).

Sustainable Energy – Without the Hot Air by David J.C. Mackay (UIT, 2008; free download at www.withouthotair. com).

The End of Nature by Bill McKibben, (second revised edition Bloomsbury, 2003).

Deep Economy: The Wealth of Communities and a Durable Future by Bill McKibben (Henry Holt, 2007).

The Meaning of the 21st Century: A Vital Blueprint for Ensuring Our Future by James Martin (Eden Project Books, 2006).

Global Warming: A Very Short Introduction by Mark Maslin (revised edition Oxford University Press, 2008).

The Limits to Growth: The 30-year Update by D.H. Meadows, Jorgen Randers and Dennis Meadows (Earthscan, 2004).

Radical Ecology: The Search for a Livable World by Carolyn Merchant (revised edition Routledge, 2005).

Contraction and Convergence: The Global Solution to Climate Change (Schumacher Briefing) by Aubrey Meyer (Green Books, 2000).

Earthy Realism: The Meaning of Gaia edited by Mary Midgley (Imprint Academic, 2007).

Confronting Climate Change: Risks, Implications and Responses edited by Irving M. Mintzer (Cambridge University Press, 1992).

Amazon Watershed by George Monbiot (Michael Joseph, 1991).

Heat: How to Stop the Planet Burning by George Monbiot (Allen Lane, 2006).

Bring on the Apocalypse: Six Arguments for Global Justice by George Monbiot (Atlantic Books, 2008).

Creating a Climate for Change edited by Susanne Moser and Lisa Dilling (Cambridge University Press, 2007).

Ecology, Community and Lifestyle: Outline of an Ecosophy by Arne Naess, (Cambridge University Press, 1990).

The Ecology of Wisdom: Writings by Arne Naess edited by Alan Drengson and Bill Devall (Counterpoint, 2008).

Shadow Cities: A Billion Squatters, a New Urban World by Robert Neuwirth (Routledge, 2004).

Environmental Values (Routledge Introductions to Environment) by John O'Neill, Alan Holland and Andrew Light (Routledge, 2007).

The Last Generation: How Nature Will Take Revenge for Man-Made Climate Change by Fred Pearce (Eden Project Books, 2006).

When the River Runs Dry: What Happens When Our Water Runs Out? by Fred Pearce (Eden Project Books, 2007).

Confessions of an Eco Sinner: Travels to Find Where My Stuff Comes From by Fred Pearce. (Eden Project Books, 2008).

The World According to Pimm: A Scientist Audits the Earth by Stuart Pimm (McGraw-Hill, 2001).

A Green History of the World by Clive Ponting (Sinclair-Stevenson, 1991; Vintage 2007).

Capitalism As If the World Matters by Jonathon Porritt (Earthscan, 2005).

Climate Change Begins at Home: Life on the Two-Way Street of Global Warming by Dave Reay (Palgrave Macmillan, 2005).

The Voice of the Earth: An Exploration of Ecopsychology by Theodore Roszak (Bantam Press, 1993; Phanes Press, 2002).

Listening to Grasshoppers: Field Notes on Democracy by Arundhati Roy (Hamish Hamilton, 2009).

Common Wealth: Economics for a Crowded Planet by Jeffrey Sachs (Allen Lane, 2008).

Do Good Lives Have to Cost the Earth? edited by Andrew Simms and Joe Smith (Constable, 2008).

The Life You Can Save: Acting Now to End World Poverty by Peter Singer (Picador, 2009).

The State of the World Atlas by Dan Smith (eighth edition Earthscan, 2008).

Red Sky at Morning: America and the Crisis of the Global Environment by James Gustave Speth (Yale University Press, 2004).

Global Warming: Personal Solutions for a Healthy Planet by Chris Spence (Palgrave Macmillan, 2005).

The Economics of Climate Change: The Stern Review by Nicholas Stern (Cambridge University Press, 2007; download at www.hm-treasury.gov.uk/stern_review_report.htm).

Blueprint for a Safer Planet/The Global Deal by Nicholas Stern (Bodley Head; PublicAffairs, 2009).

I Count: Your Step-by-Step Guide to Climate Bliss by Stop Climate Chaos, (Penguin Books, 2006).

Kyoto2: How to Manage the Global Greenhouse by Oliver Tickell (Zed Books, 2008).

Africa in Crisis: The Causes and Cures of Environmental Bankruptcy by Lloyd Timberlake (Earthscan, 1985).

When the Bough Breaks: Our Children, Our Environment by Lloyd Timberlake and Laura Thomas (Earthscan, 1990).

The Urgency of Now by Lloyd Timberlake (Still Pictures Moving Words, 2009).

The Hot Topic: How to Tackle Global Warming and Still Keep the Lights On by Gabrielle Walker and Sir David King (Bloomsbury, 2009).

Only One Earth by Barbara Ward and René Dubois, (André Deutsch, 1972).

The World Without Us by Alan Weisman (Virgin Books, 2007).

The Future of Life by Edward O. Wilson (Knopf, 2002).

Our Common Future by the World Commission on Environment and Development (OUP, 1987).

State of the World by the Worldwatch Institute (annual report).

Vital Signs: The Trends That Are Shaping Our Future by the Worldwatch Institute (annual report).

Selected fiction

Night Train by Martin Amis (Jonathan Cape, 1997).

The Drowned World by J.G. Ballard (Victor Gollanz, 1962; Harper Perennial, 2006).

The Drought by J.G. Ballard (Jonathan Cape, 1965; Harper Perennial, 2008).

State of Fear by Michael Crichton (Harper Collins, 2004).

The Road by Cormac McCarthy (Knopf/Picador, 2006).

Ishmael: An Adventure of the Mind and Spirit by Daniel Quinn (Bantam, 1992).

The Day After Tomorrow by Whitley Strieber (Gollancz, 2004).

Selected films (by title)

An Inconvenient Truth, Davis Guggenheim, Al Gore (Lawrence Bender/Participant Productions, 2006).

Food, Inc, Robert Kenner (Magnolia Pictures/Participant Media/River Road Entertainment, 2008).

Hard Rain, Mark Edwards, Bob Dylan (Still Pictures Moving Words, 2009).

Home, Yann Arthus-Bertrand (Elzévir Films/EuropaCorp, 2009).

Ice Age series, Chris Wedge, Carlos Saldanha, Mike Thurmeier (20th Century Fox/Blue Sky Studios, 2002–9).

Super Size Me, Morgan Spurlock (Kathbur Pictures/The Con/Studio On Hudson, 2004).

The 11th Hour, Nadia Conners, Leila Conners Petersen, Leonardo DiCaprio (Appian Way/Green Hour/Tree Media Group, 2007).

The Age of Stupid, Franny Armstrong (Spanner Films/Passion Pictures, 2009).

The Cove, Louie Psihoyos (Roadside Attractions/Oceanic Preservation Society/Participant Media, 2009).

The Day After Tomorrow, Roland Emmerich (20th Century Fox, 2004).

The End of the Line, Rupert Murray, Charles Clover (Dartmouth Films/Arcane Pictures/Calm Productions/Fish Film Company, 2009).

Organizations

Use these links to keep track of what governments, international agencies and advocacy groups are saying about the issues in Hard Rain.

1sky
www.1sky.org

11th Hour Action
http://11thhouraction.com

350.org
www.350.org

Act on CO$_2$
http://campaigns2.direct.gov.uk/actonco2/home.html

Act on Copenhagen
www.actoncopenhagen.decc.gov.uk

African Development Bank Group
www.afdb.org

Age of Stupid
www.ageofstupid.net

Alliance for Climate Education
www.climateeducation.org

Alliance for Climate Protection
www.climateprotect.org
(see also *Climate Crisis, Climate Project, Repower Amercia, This Is Reality* and *We Can Solve It*)

Alliance of Religions and Conservation (ARC)
www.arcworld.org

Alliance to Save Energy
www.ase.org

Amazon Watch
www.amazonwatch.org

American Association for the
Advancement of Science
www.aaas.org

Amnesty International
www.amnesty.org

An Inconvenient Truth
(see Climate Crisis)

ARKive
www.arkive.org

Artists Project Earth
www.apeuk.org

Asian Development Bank.
www.adb.org

Association for the Advancement of
Sustainability in Higher Education
www.aashe.org

Bill and Melinda Gates Foundation
www.gatesfoundation.org

Billion Tree Campaign
(see UNEP Billion Tree Campaign)

BobDylan.com
www.bobdylan.com

Botanic Gardens Conservation
International
www.bgci.org.uk

California Academy of Sciences
www.calacademy.org

Cambridge Programme for
Sustainability Leadership
www.cpsl.cam.ac.uk

Camp for Climate Action
www.climatecamp.org.uk

Canadian Parks and Wilderness Society
www.cpaws.org

CAN International
(see Climate Action Network)

Cape Farewell
www.capefarewell.com

Carbon Commentary
www.carboncommentary.com

Care for the Wild International
www.careforthewild.com

Carnegie Institution for Science
www.ciw.edu

Center for Media and Democracy
www.prwatch.org

Center for Resource Solutions
www.resource-solutions.org

Centre for Social Justice
www.centreforsocialjustice.org.uk

Centre for Social Markets
www.csmworld.org

Christian Aid
www.christianaid.org.uk

CICERO (Center for International
Climate and Environmental Research
– Oslo)
www.cicero.uio.no

Circle Up Now
www.circleupnow.org

Clean Air Foundation
www.cleanairfoundation.org

Climate Action Network (CAN
International)
www.climatenetwork.org

Climate Ark
www.climateark.org

Climate Care
www.climatecare.org

Climate Change TV
(see Responding to Climate Change)

Climate Counts
www.climatecounts.org

Climate Crisis/An Inconvenient Truth
www.climatecrisis.net

Climate Group
www.theclimategroup.org

Climate Project
www.theclimateproject.org

ClimateWire.org
www.climatewire.org

Clinton Climate Initiative
www.clintonfoundation.org

CO_2 Science
www.co2science.org

Comparative Research Programme
on Poverty
www.crop.org

Congress.org
www.congress.org

Conservation International
www.conservation.org

Convention on Biological Diversity
www.biodiv.org

Cool Planet 2009
www.coolplanet2009.org

Copenhagen Climate Conference/
COP15
(see *United Nations Climate Change
Conference 2009*)

Ctrl.Alt.Shift
www.ctrlaltshift.co.uk

David Suzuki Foundation
www.davidsuzuki.org

Debt AIDS Trade Africa
www.data.org

Development Gateway Foundation
www.developmentgateway.org

Earth from the Air/Earth from Above
(see *Yann Arthus-Bertrand.org*)

Earth Institute
www.earthinstitute.columbia.edu

Earth Policy Institute
www.earth-policy.org

Earth Restoration Service/Restore the
Earth
www.earthrestorationservice.org
www.restore-earth.org

Earthscan
www.earthscan.co.uk

Earthwatch Institute
www.earthwatch.org

EC Commission Institute for Energy
http://ie.jrc.ec.europa.eu

Ecotricity
www.ecotricity.co.uk

Eden Project
www.edenproject.com

Edge of Existence
www.edgeofexistence.org

Eldis Gateway to Development
Information
www.eldis.org

Encyclopedia of Life
www.eol.org

End of the Line
http://endoftheline.com

Energy Action Coalition
www.energyactioncoalition.org

Energy Saving Trust
www.est.org.uk

Enough's Enough
www.enoughsenough.org

Envirolink
www.envirolink.org

Environmental Association for
Universities and Colleges
www.eauc.org.uk

Environmental Concern
www.wetland.org

Environmental Defense
www.environmentaldefense.org

Environmental Health News
www.environmentalhealthnews.org

Environmentalists for Nuclear Energy
www.ecelo.org

Environmental Media Services
www.ems.org

European Commission Environment
Directorate
europa.eu.int/comm/environment

Fair Trade Foundation
www.fairtrade.org.uk

Food and Agriculture Organization of
the United Nations
www.fao.org
(see also *World Food Summit*)

Food Democracy Now
www.fooddemocracynow.org

Focus the Nation (a Green House
Network project)
www.focusthenation.org

Forum for the Future
www.forumforthefuture.org.uk

Friends of the Earth
www.foe.co.uk
www.foei.org

G8
www.g8.utoronto.ca

G20
www.g20.org

Global Call to Action against Poverty
(GCAP)
www.whiteband.org

Global Commons Institute
www.gci.org.uk

Global Cool Foundation
www.globalcool.org

Global Environment Facility
www.gefweb.org

Global Footprint Network
www.footprintnetwork.org

Global Humanitarian Forum Geneva
www.ghf-ge.org

Global Humanitarian Organization
www.globalhumanitarian.net

Global Leadership for Climate Action
www.globalclimateaction.org

Global Oneness Project
www.globalonenessproject.org

Global Warming 101 (a Will Steger
Foundation initiative)
www.globalwarming101.com

Global Warming International Center
www.globalwarming.net

GLOBE International
www.globeinternational.org

Goddard Institute for Space Studies
www.giss.nasa.gov

Good Planet Foundation
www.goodplanet.org
(see also Yann Arthus-Bertrand.org)

Google Earth
http://earth.google.com

Grameen Bank
www.grameen-info.org

Gorbachev Foundation
www.gorby.ru

GreenBiz
www.greenbiz.com

Green Belt Movement
www.greenbeltmovement.org

Green Car Congress
www.greencarcongress.com

Green Empowerment
www.greenempowerment.org

Green House Network
www.greenhousenet.org

Green Nexxus
www.greennexxus.com
(see also One Million Acts of Green)

Green Options Media
www.greenoptions.com

Greenpeace
www.greenpeace.org

Green TV
www.green.tv

Grist
www.grist.org

Gurukula Botanical Sanctuary
www.gbsanctuary.org

Hard Rain Project
www.hardrainproject.com

Healthbridge Foundation of Canada
www.healthbridge.ca

Impossible2Possible
www.impossible2possible.com

Inconvenient Youth (a Climate Project
partner)
www.inconvenientyouth.org

Institute for Policy Studies
www.ips-dc.org

Intergovernmental Panel on Climate
Change
www.ipcc.ch

International Emissions Trading
Association
www.ieta.org

International Energy Agency
www.iea.org

International Fund for Agricultural
Development
www.ifad.org

International Forum on Globalization
www.ifg.org

International Glaciological Society
www.igsoc.org

International Institute for Environment
and Development
www.iied.org

International Institute for Sustainable
Development
www.iisd.org

International Monetary Fund
www.imf.org

International Youth Climate Movement
www.facebook.com/youthclimate.org
www.itsgettinghotinhere.org

Internews
www.internews.org

It's Getting Hot in Here
(see International Youth Climate
Movement)

Islands First
www.islandsfirst.org

IUCN Red List
(see World Conservation Union)

Kyoto2
www.kyoto2.org

Kyoto Protocol
(see United Nations Framework
Convention on Climate Change)

Leonardo DiCaprio Foundation
www.leonardodicaprio.org

Live Earth
www.liveearth.org

MacArthur Foundation
www.macfound.org

Médécins Sans Frontières
www.msf.org

Millennium Ecosystem Assessment
www.maweb.org

NASA
www.nasa.gov

National Oceanic & Atmospheric
Administration/NOAA National
Environmental Satellite, Date and
Information Service
www.noaa.gov
www.nesdis.noaa.gov

National Wildlife Federation
www.nwf.org

Natural Resources Defense Council
www.nrdc.org

Natural Step
www.naturalstep.org

Nature Conservancy
www.nature.org

New Economics Foundation
www.neweconomics.org

Ocean Alliance
www.oceanalliance.org

Ocean Project/World Oceans Day
www.theoceanproject.org

Ocean River Institute
www.oceanriver.org

Oceanic Preservation Society
www.opsociety.org

Optimum Population Trust
www.optimumpopulation.org

One
www.one.org

One Million Acts of Green
www.greennexxus.com/omaog/us

One Planet Living
www.oneplanetliving.org

Open Society Institute/Soros
Foundations Network
www.soros.org

Organic Consumers Association
www.organicconsumers.org

Organisation for Economic Co-operation
and Development
www.oecd.org

Oxfam
www.oxfam.org

Peaceful Uprising
www.peacefuluprising.org

People and the Planet
www.peopleandplanet.net

Pew Center on Global Climate Change
www.pewclimate.org

Plane Stupid
www.planestupid.com

Planet Ark
www.planetark.com

Plantlife International
www.plantlife.org.uk

Post Carbon Institute
www.postcarbon.org

Potsdam Institute for Climate Impact
Research
www.pik-potsdam.de

Powershift '09 (an Energy Action
Coalition project)
www.powershift09.org

Poverty Action Lab
www.povertyactionlab.org

Prince of Wales Rainforest Project
www.rainforestSOS.org

Project 90 by 2030
www.90x2030.org.za

Rainforest Action Network
www.ran.org

Red Cross/Red Crescent
www.icrc.org
www.ifrc.org

Repower America (an Alliance for
Climate Protection project)
www.repoweramerica.org

Resources for the Future/Weathervane
www.rff.org
www.rff.org/wv

Responding to Climate Change/Climate
Change TV
www.rtcc.org
www.climate-change.tv

Restore the Earth
(see Earth Restoration Service)

Road to Copenhagen
www.roadtocopenhagen.org

Royal Society
www.royalsoc.ac.uk

Schumacher College
www.schumachercollege.org.uk

Scottish Action on Climate Change
www.soac.org.uk

Scottish Parliament
www.scottish.parliament.uk

Scripps Institution of Oceanography
www.sio.ucsd.edu

Seal the Deal
www.sealthedeal2009.org

Sierra Club
www.sierraclub.org

Slum Dewellers International
www.sdinet.co.za

Soil Association
www.soilassociation.org

Solar Aid
www.solar-aid.org

Soros Foundations Network
(see Open Society Institute)

Stephan Schmidheiny
www.stephanschmidheiny.net

Stern Review
www.hm-treasury.gov.uk/stern_review_
report.htm

Still Pictures
www.stillpictures.com

Stockholm International Water Institute
www.siwi.org

Stop Climate Chaos
www.stopclimatechaos.org

Stop Global Warming
www.stopglobalwarming.org

Survival International
www.survival-international.org

SustainAbility
www.sustainability.com

Sustain West Cork
www.sustainwestcork.com

Susty
www.susty.com

Tällberg Foundation and Forum
www.tallbergfoundation.org

Taking II Global
www.tigweb.org

TckTckTck: Time for Climate Justice
www.tcktcktck.org

Team for Nature and Wildlife Nepal
www.tnwnepal.org

This Is Reality (an Alliance for Climate
Protection project)
www.thisisreality.org

Together.com
www.together.com

Transition Towns
www.transitiontowns.org

Treehugger.com
www.treehugger.com

Tyndall Centre for Climate Change
Research
www.tyndall.ac.uk

UK Committee on Climate Change
www.theccc.org.uk

UK Climate Projections
http://ukclimateprojections.defra.gov.uk/

UK Department of Energy and Climate
Change
www.decc.gov.uk

UK Department for Environment, Food
and Rural Affairs
www.defra.gov.uk

UK Department for International
Development
www.dfid.gov.uk

UK Department for Transport
www.dft.gov.uk

UK Directgov
www.direct.gov.uk

UK Conservative Party
www.conservatives.com

UK Green Party
www.greenparty.org.uk

UK Labour Party
www.labour.org.uk

UK Liberal Democrats
www.libdems.org.uk

UK Prime Minister's Office
www.number10.gov.uk

UK Sustainable Development
Commission
www.sd-commission.org.uk

Union of Concerned Scientists
www.ucsusa.org

United Nations Children's Fund
(UNICEF)
www.unicef.org

United Nations Climate Change
Conference 2009
http://en.cop15.dk

United Nations Convention to Combat Desertification
www.unccd.int

United Nations Development Programme
www.undp.org

United Nations Educational, Scientific and Cultural Organization
www.unesco.org

United Nations Environment Programme
www.unep.org

United Nations Food and Agriculture Organization
(see Food and Agriculture Organization of the United Nations)

UNEP Billion Tree Campaign
www.unep.org/billiontreecampaign

United Nations Framework Convention on Climate Change
www.unfccc.int

United Nations Millennium Development Goals
www.un.org/millenniumgoals

United Nations Population Fund
www.unfpa.org

US Climate Action Partnership
www.us-cap.org

US Climate Change Science Program
www.climatescience.gov

US Climate Change Technology Program
www.climatetechnology.gov

US Climate Task Force
www.climatetaskforce.org

US Democratic Party
www.democrats.com

US Environmental Protection Agency
www.epa.gov

US Geological Survey
www.usgs.gov

US Global Change Research Program
www.globalchange.gov

US global climate change policy
www.state.gov/g/oes/climate

US House of Representatives
www.house.gov
(see also www.congress.org)

US President's office
www.whitehouse.gov

US Republican National Committee
www.gop.com

US Senate
www.senate.org

Water Aid
www.wateraid.org

We Can Solve It (an Alliance for Climate Protection project)
www.wecansolveit.org

Weathervane
(see Resources for the Future)

Welsh Assembly
http://wales.gov.uk

WILD Foundation/World Wilderness Congress
www.wild.org

Will Steger Foundation
www.willstegerfoundation.org

Women's Environment and Development Organization
www.wcdo.org

World Bank
www.worldbank.org

World Business Council for Sustainable Development
www.wbcsd.org

WorldChanging
www.worldchanging.com

World Conservation Union/IUCN Red List
www.iucn.org
www.iucnredlist.org

World Development Movement
www.wdm.org.uk

World Food Summit
www.fao.org/WFS/homepage.htm

World Health Organization
www.who.int

World Meteorological Organization
www.wmo.ch

World Oceans Project
(see Ocean Project)

World Resources Institute
www.wri.org

World Trade Organization
www.wto.org

World Water Council/World Water Forum
www.worldwatercouncil.org

World Wilderness Congress
(see WILD Foundation)

Worldwatch Institute
www.worldwatch.org

WWF
www.panda.org

Yale School of Forestry & Environmental Studies
www.environment.yale.edu

Yann Arthus-Bertrand.org
www.yannarthusbertrand.org
(see also *Good Planet Foundation*)

Festivals

2000 Trees
www.twothousandtreesfestival.co.uk

Benicàssim (Spain)
www.fiberfib.com

Bestival
www.bestival.net

Big Chill
www.bigchill.net

Big Green Gathering
www.big-green-gathering.com

Burning Man (USA)
www.burningman.com

Creamfields
www.creamfields.com

Croissant Neuf
www.partyneuf.co.uk

Dragonfly (Sweden)
www.dragonflyfestival.org

Electric Picnic (Ireland)
www.electricpicnic.ie

Glastonbury
www.glastonburyfestivals.co.uk

Global Gathering
www.globalgathering.co.uk

Greenbelt
www.greenbelt.org.uk

Green Festival (USA)
www.greenfestivals.org

Green Man
www.thegreenmanfestival.co.uk

Isle of White
www.isleofwightfestival.com

Latitude
www.latitudefestival.co.uk

Leeds
www.leedsfestival.com

Lodestar
www.lodestarfestival.com

Lowlands (Netherlands)
www.lowlands.nl

Moondance Jam (USA)
www.moondancejam.com

Musicport
www.musicportfestival.com

Nowhere (Spain)
www.goingnowhere.org

Oxegen (Ireland)
www.oxegen.ie

Pinkpop (Netherlands)
www.pinkpop.nl

Rainbow Serpent (Australia)
www.rainbowserpent.net

Reading
www.readingfestival.com

Reeperbahn (Germany)
www.reeperbahnfestival.com

Rock Ness
www.rockness.co.uk

Rock Werchter (Belgium)
www.rockwerchter.be

Roskilde (Denmark)
www.roskilde-festival.dk

Secret Garden Party
www.secretgardenparty.com

Shambala
www.shambalafestival.org

Sunrise Celebration
www.sunrisecelebration.com

Symbiosis Gathering (USA)
www.symbiosisgathering.com

Sziget (Hungary)
www.sziget.hu

T in the Park
www.tinthepark.com

V Festival
www.vfestival.com

Waveform
www.waveformfestival.com

Weyfest
www.weyfest.co.uk

Wickerman
www.thewickermanfestival.co.uk

WOMAD
www.womad.org

Can't find the festival you were looking for?
Try www.welovefestivals.com

Newspapers, journals and news sites

American Scientist
www.americanscientist.org

BBC
http://news.bbc.co.uk

Boston Globe
www.boston.com

Christian Science Monitor
www.csmonitor.com

Counter Punch
www.counterpunch.org

Ecologist
www.theecologist.org

Geographical
www.geographical.co.uk

Green Futures
www.greenfutures.org.uk

Guardian
www.guardian.co.uk

Huffington Post
www.huffingtonpost.com

Independent
www.independent.co.uk

Los Angeles Times
www.latimes.com

Mother Jones
www.motherjones.com

National Geographic
www.nationalgeographic.com

Nature
www.nature.com

New Internationalist
www.newint.org

New Left Review
www.newleftreview.org

The New Republic
www.tnr.com

New Scientist
www.newscientist.com

New York Times
www.nytimes.com

New York Review of Books
www.nybooks.com

Observer
www.observer.guardian.co.uk

Resurgence
www.resurgence.org

Salon.com
www.salon.com

Sanctuary Asia
www.sanctuaryasia.com

Scientific American
www.sciam.com

Utne Reader
www.utne.com

Washington Post
www.washingtonpost.com

We welcome information about relevant books, films, organizations, festivals and news sources so we can update future editions of this book and our website. Please contact Mark Reynolds: mark.reynolds@hardrainproject.com